The Answers Book for Kids

Volume 2

22 Questions on Dinosaurs and the Flood of Noah

Nineteenth Printing: August 2022

Master Books
P.O. Box 726
Green Forest, AR 72638

Master Books® is a division of the New Leaf Publishing Group, Inc.

Printed in China

Cover Design by Rebekah Krall
Interior Design by Terry White

ISBN 13: 978-0-89051-527-3
ISBN 13: 978-1-61458-284-7 (digital)

Library of Congress number: 2008929454

All Scripture references are New King James Version unless otherwise noted.

Please visit our website for other great titles: www.masterbooks.com

When you see this icon, there will be related Scripture references noted for parents to use in answering their children's, and even their own, questions.

For Parents and Teachers

Look now at the behemoth, which I made along with you; he eats grass like an ox.
See now, his strength is in his hips, and his power is in his stomach muscles.
He moves his tail like a cedar; the sinews of his thighs are tightly knit.
His bones are like beams of bronze, his ribs like bars of iron (Job 40:15–18).

Dear Moms and Dads:

As I have traveled the world these past 30+ years, I realize that dinosaurs are used more than almost anything else to indoctrinate children (and teens and adults) into believing the idea of millions of years of earth history.

Many Christian parents have been unable to counter this indoctrination because they don't know how to answer questions about dinosaurs, the fossil record, and the age of the earth. They cannot defend biblical authority and the Genesis history that is foundational to the rest of the Bible.

Sadly, when children don't get biblical answers, many of them are put on a slippery slide to unbelief — doubting the first part of the Bible (Genesis). This can ultimately lead to their doubt and unbelief of the rest of the Bible.

As parents, we are admonished to make known to our children the wonderful works of God — *"that the generation to come might know them, the children who would be born, that they may arise and declare them to their children, that they may set their hope in God, and not forget the works of God"* (Psalm 78:6–7). What an awesome privilege and responsibility God has given us!

My prayer is that this book will give crucial answers to assist you in building within your children a foundation to know and trust God's Word — right from the very first verse — and that one day they may put their faith in our Savior — the Creator of the universe — Jesus Christ.

Ken Ham
President/CEO, Answers in Genesis

Question: Were people different before the Flood than they are today?

Olivia K.

Age 11 — Australia

4

Answer:

Now the whole earth had one language and one speech. . . . "Come, let Us go down and there confuse their language, that they may not understand one another's speech" (Genesis 11:1, 7).

All people are of one race (descended from Adam), created in the image of God. But Olivia, I'm sure you see unique differences in people, even in your neighborhood. The Bible tells us what happened between Noah and today that caused such differences in people to arise. After the Flood, the people became prideful in their own efforts and disobeyed God's command to spread out over the earth. They built the Tower of Babel to worship the heavens instead of worshiping God.

So God confused their language — resulting in different language groups being formed. They could no longer understand one another. This caused them to move away from each other. And as the various groups became more and more separated, minor differences in groups arose as a result of the differing combinations of human genes. So, yes, I believe the people were probably a bit different back before the Flood because they spoke the same language and looked more similar than humans do today — but we are still humans belonging to one race.

Genesis 11:1–9

Question: Did Noah take dinosaurs on the ark?

Joy B.

Age 10 — Michigan, USA

6

Answer:

And of every living thing of all flesh you shall bring two of every sort into the ark, to keep them alive with you; they shall be male and female (Genesis 6:19).

Can you even imagine it? Dinosaurs on the ark? It is so very cool to think about. And we can be *sure* they were there because the Bible tells us that every kind of air-breathing, land-dwelling animal went aboard. Now, Noah did not know of the word dinosaur back then. In fact, that word was made up in 1841 to describe land animals found that had very unique bone structures, uncommon to other animals. Dinosaur literally means "Terrible Lizard."

But we do know what God tells us — that *all* the kinds of land animals were on the ark. Well, that just *had* to include the dinosaur kinds, too!

Genesis 6:19–20, 7:14

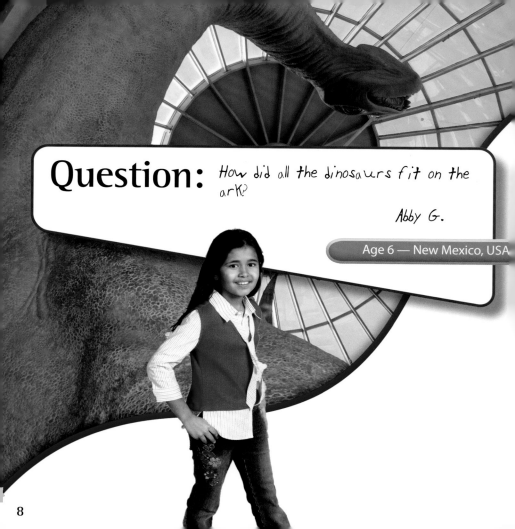

Question: How did all the dinosaurs fit on the ark?

Abby G.

Age 6 — New Mexico, USA

8

Answer:

And this is how you shall make it: The length of the ark shall be three hundred cubits, its width fifty cubits, and its height thirty cubits (Genesis 6:15).

Abby, your question is often asked by people a lot older than six! First of all, God told Noah how big to make the ark (see our verse). You might ask, what is a cubit? I believe the cubit that was used was about 20 inches long . . . and that would make the ark as long as one and a half football fields — about 510 feet (155 meters) — as tall as a 4-story building — about 45 feet (14 meters) — and about 85 feet (23 meters) wide! It was really big! Now another thing is that although there are hundreds of names of dinosaurs, there were probably only about 50 actual kinds. So, there may have only been a total of 100 dinosaurs on the ark. That still seems like a lot, doesn't it?

But, did you know that most dinosaurs were actually quite small? In fact, the average size of a dinosaur is the size of a sheep. (Some were as small as chickens!) And for the few dinosaurs that grew large, it would make sense that God would send smaller young adults. You know, after looking at all of these facts, I think there was plenty of room on the ark for the dinosaurs and all the other animals God sent to survive the Flood.

Genesis 1:25, 7:14

Question: How did Noah get two of every sea animal on the ark?

Heidi C.

Age 10 — Ohio, USA

Answer:

Of the birds after their kind, of animals after their kind, and of every creeping thing of the earth after its kind, two of every kind will come to you to keep them alive (Genesis 6:20).

So, did Noah need a great big aquarium on board the ark? No, not at all! See our Bible verse, Heidi? It doesn't mention sea animals, does it? Noah didn't need to build an aquarium because the ark was sailing in one . . . and it was plenty big!

We know that many sea animals were killed in the Flood because most of the fossils we have are of sea creatures. The Flood was hard on them because the water was rough, the mud and sediment buried them, and the water temperatures and amount of salt were changing. But God allowed enough of them to survive the Flood so that we still have all the sea creature kinds we see today.

Genesis 6:17, 7:15, 7:22

11

Question: Did Noah have to estimate how much food to gather or did God tell him?

Heidi C.

Age 10 — Ohio, USA

12

Answer:

And you shall take for yourself of all food that is eaten, and you shall gather it to yourself; and it shall be food for you and for them (Genesis 6:21).

Often we wish the Bible would give us more details, don't we? But, we know from our verse that God said to take food on board. It could be that God told Noah exactly what to take, but it just wasn't written down. It is also possible that Noah, who was almost 500 years old when God told him about the Flood, knew a lot about animals, like what and how much they needed to eat. Noah was, after all, very intelligent — smart enough to build the ark.

The animals couldn't have been as active while they were on the ark. You know, no more running, playing, swimming, chasing each other (they were on a boat, after all). So, I'm thinking they wouldn't have needed as much food to stay healthy and keep their bodies functioning properly. Again, we don't know what Noah did for sure, but I'm confident that Noah knew exactly what to bring and exactly how much to bring.

Genesis 7:5, 8:1

13

Question: How did Noah keep the animals on the ark from eating each other and his family?

Chase P.

Age 8— South Carolina, USA

14

Answer:

Then God remembered Noah, and every living thing, and all the animals that were with him in the ark. And God made a wind to pass over the earth, and the waters subsided (Genesis 8:1).

Our Bible verse tells us that God remembered Noah. God promised to deliver Noah and his family through the Flood. God was looking after Noah, and God was in control of every detail of Noah's voyage.

One possible answer to your question is that God could have miraculously stopped animals from eating each other. There is another possibility. We know that before sin, animals only ate vegetation. By the time of the Flood, a number of animals may have become vicious because of the effects of sin. But we notice today that even with animals like wolves — which are of the dog kind — there are other dogs that are not vicious. So God could have chosen the more friendly ones to represent a kind. God could also have supernaturally caused the animals to hibernate much of the time. And Noah no doubt built cages or rooms with doors to keep the animals from roaming the ark and possibly hurting other animals.

It is good to think about these things — it helps us to see there are many possible answers to your question.

But we can be sure that as God brought the different kinds of animals to Noah, He knew what was in store. He sent the animals to the ark and He would see that the animals and the people would survive the long trip together.

Genesis 1:29–30, 9:3

15

Question: Why did God make meat-eating animals? Why are they not still plant-eaters?

Nickie H.

Age 7 — Florida, USA

16

Answer:

Also, to every beast of the earth, to every bird of the air, and to everything that creeps on the earth, in which there is life, I have given every green herb for food (Genesis 1:30).

Once again, we can look to the Bible to give us the answer to our questions, Nickie. Originally, God did not create any meat-eating animals. All the animals were vegetarian, just like our Bible verse says. They were given every green herb (plants, grass, fruits, vegetables) for food. Now, eating all of those plants and vegetables and fruit might not be so easy without a good, sharp knife. And I believe that is why some animals have big, pointed, scary-looking teeth (well, scary in a fallen world)! After all, even some animals with sharp teeth today don't necessarily eat only meat. For instance, the panda has very sharp teeth and yet for the most part it still pretty much eats bamboo plants.

Because of sin, violence and death came into the world. Now, many animals eat other animals. But the Bible tells us that one day Jesus will restore His creation to its perfect state. There will no longer be sickness or death, and animals won't eat each other. What a glorious day that will be!

Genesis 6:13; Romans 6:23; Revelation 21:1–4

Question:

Why did God allow some creatures to go extinct?

Ben D.

Age 10 — Canada

18

Answer:

. . . but of the tree of the knowledge of good and evil you shall not eat, for in the day that you eat of it you shall surely die (Genesis 2:17).

Ben, we know that some animals are extinct and some are on the endangered list, meaning they may soon become extinct. We need to understand that it is not God's fault the animals are going extinct. It's actually our fault because we sinned against God. When God first created the universe, He said it was all "very good." It was a place with no death or suffering anywhere! But Adam and Eve's disobedience to God brought death into the world — and the whole universe began to change because of God's judgment on our sin.

This was a very sad day because the very good universe now began to run down. Sin changed everything. With it came death, sickness, and suffering. Changes occurred in the weather, the food supply, the behavior of people, and the behavior of animals. These (and other) changes have contributed to why many animals have gone extinct.

But remember the good news! God promises to one day restore everything back to a perfect world where animals will no longer go extinct and people will no longer sin against God's commands.

Genesis 1:31; Romans 5:12; Psalm 33:20–22

Question: What happened to the ark once Noah, his family, and the animals got off?

Cameron P.

Age 10— South Carolina, USA

FOR SALE
NOAH 454

20

Answer:

Then God spoke to Noah, saying, "Go out of the ark, you and your wife, and your sons and your sons' wives with you" (Genesis 8:15–16).

The Flood destroyed everything on earth. Noah and his family remained in the ark while waiting for the waters to subside and the ground to dry out. But we know that they eventually left the ark. (I like to think about what a relief it must have been for them to breathe the fresh air and stand on solid ground again!)

The Bible mentions that Noah lived in a tent. It is very possible that Noah brought tents on the ark so he and his family would have places to live once the Flood was over. With everything else destroyed, and as Noah's family grew, the ark may have provided building materials for the homes and other buildings they would all eventually need. It may have decayed, been used as firewood, or destroyed by other means. If the ark did survive (and there is no real evidence it has) — the wood would have to be preserved in some way, like being petrified.

This is one of those things, Cameron, the Bible doesn't clearly tell us.

Genesis 8:4–16

Question:

After the Flood, were there any buildings left?

Joanne C.

Age 8 — Arkansas, USA

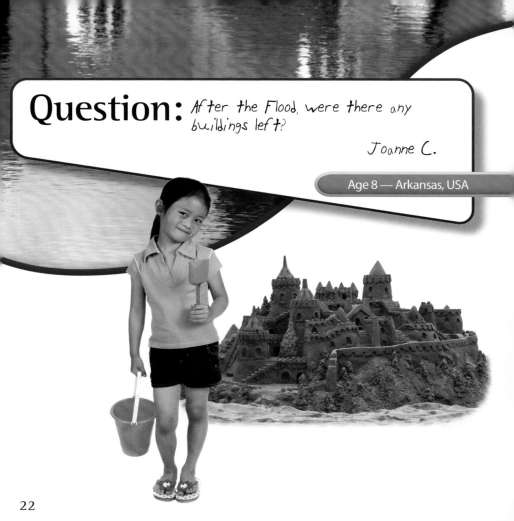

22

Answer:

So the LORD said, "I will destroy man whom I have created from the face of the earth, both man and beast, creeping thing and birds of the air . . . " (Genesis 6:7).

For the answer to this question, we're going to get a little lesson in geology (the study of rocks, canyons, and mountains). If you visit the Grand Canyon, there is what we call "basement" rocks that are a mile down into the canyon. These rocks are amazing in that it looks as though someone took a really sharp knife and just sliced the earth right off. On top of that you see layers of rocks, sand, and mud that were laid down by water right over the "basement" rocks. This gives some understanding of how devastating the Flood really was. How it just wiped out the surface of the earth. The Flood was cataclysmic — it was dreadful, tragic, a disaster, devastating. It destroyed everything and everyone on earth just as it was intended to do. So there wouldn't have been any buildings left from before the Flood.

Genesis 7:4; Luke 17:27

23

Question: Did we use dinosaurs for transportation?

Joy B.

Age 10 —Michigan, USA

24

Answer:

For every kind of beast and bird, of reptile and creature of the sea, is tamed and has been tamed by mankind (James 3:7).

I know the Bible doesn't specifically address this question, but Joy, we can use the reasoning skills God gave us and His Word to come up with an answer. We see and hear about all sorts of animals being tamed by man. In fact, from our Bible verse it appears that we shouldn't be surprised that animals can be tamed. I can think of many animals that have been tamed to work for humans. There are elephants, tigers, bears, horses, dogs (of course), lions, camels, birds, dolphins, walruses, even the great killer whale, and a lot more! This is one of those things that is just fun to think about, isn't it? So, why not some of the dinosaurs? Who knows what they were doing? It seems to me we should at least allow the possibility that some could have been tamed to help with transportation, maybe even farming, hauling heavy loads (the strong ones!), and other things. After all, some dragon legends from China tell us that dragons (dinosaurs?) were used to pull the emperor's chariots.

Genesis 2:19–20

25

Question:

Did Noah have to search for all the animals or did they come by themselves? How did they know they had to come to the ark?

Cheyenne

Age 11 — Pennsylvania, USA

26

Answer:

…two of every kind will come to you to keep them alive (Genesis 6:20).

Cheyenne, the simple answer according to our Bible verse is no, Noah did not have to search the world for the animals because God commanded them to come to the ark. But I would like to explain a bit further so we can see how great our Creator God really is. There are several instances in the Bible where God uses animals to do His bidding. Like when God sent the big fish to swallow Jonah, who did not want to obey. And what about God commanding the ravens to feed Elijah after God sent him out to the wilderness? You see, God is the Creator; He is powerful, mighty, and great. And He clearly chose which animals would join Noah and then He commanded them to go . . . and they obeyed. After all, God is the Creator, and they had to obey their Creator (as we need to obey the Creator — the Lord Jesus).

Genesis 6:20, 7:8–9

27

Question: Where did all the water go after the Flood?

Brenna & Kennis B.

Ages 12 and 7 — Kansas, USA

Answer:

The mountains rose, the valleys sank down to the place that you appointed for them (Psalm 104:8 ESV).

Did you know that if the mountains and oceans were leveled off there would be enough water on the earth right now to cover it to a depth of about two miles? Some Bible scholars believe that our Bible verse here describes how God ended the Flood. The mountains rose up and the Flood waters went down where the ocean basins formed. Even evolutionists talk about the mountains being raised up like this, but they believe it happened over a long, long time. We believe that God did it very quickly at the end of the Flood. (By the way, that's why we find so many sea fossils near the top of mountains. Makes sense, doesn't it?) So, where is the water? I believe it is all still here. Did you realize that three-fourths of the earth is still covered with water?! The next time you go to the beach and watch God's powerful ocean, remember you're looking at the waters that once covered the entire earth during the time of the Flood!

Genesis 8:21, 9:11; 2 Peter 2:5

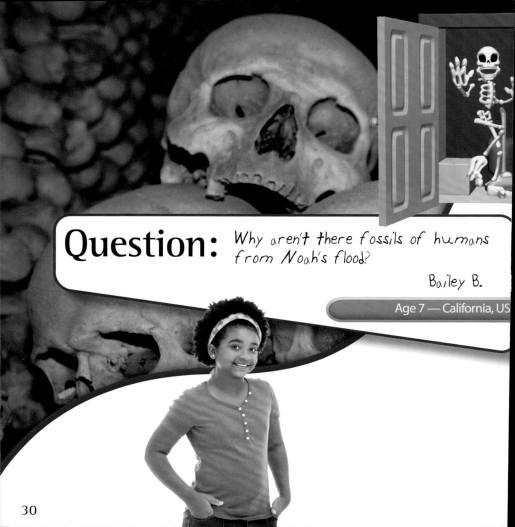

Question:

Why aren't there fossils of humans from Noah's flood?

Bailey B.

Age 7 — California, US

Answer:

So the LORD said, "I will destroy man whom I have created from the face of the earth, both man and beast, creeping thing and birds of the air, for I am sorry that I have made them" (Genesis 6:7).

Most people don't realize there are actually very few fossils of vertebrates (animals that have backbones). Almost all of the fossils ever found have been marine organisms, snails, corals, plants, and insects. In order to become a fossil, a plant or animal needs to be quickly and completely buried. It seems that humans caught in this terrible Flood would try to save themselves any way possible. It is probable that as the Flood rose, humans continued to seek higher ground. As the humans and animals died, many would float and eventually sink — only to be washed away at the end of the Flood, when the mountains rose and the waters rushed off of the earth. Also, there were only two humans to start with — but lots of different animal kinds. So one would expect to find a lot more animal fossils than humans. However, there may be some human fossils somewhere in the world — after all, scientists have dug up very little of the fossil record.

Matthew 24:39; Psalm 29:10

31

Question: Are dinosaurs still alive today? Has anybody ever taken a picture of a dinosaur?

Sawyer P.

Age 7— South Carolina, USA

32

Answer:

Look now at the behemoth, which I made along with you...
(Job 40:15–18).

Well, Sawyer, I haven't seen a photograph of a live dinosaur. (It would be cool, though!) But we have something even better than a photo. We have a description from God, our infinite Creator. In our Bible verse God describes a very large, unique animal — one that evidently was living with Job. Now Job didn't have a camera, he couldn't take a photo, so God made sure we'd know just what one of these amazing animals (the dinosaur) looked like. And there's another thing. We do have something called petroglyphs. These are drawings that people carved long ago on rocks. Some of these petroglyphs look a lot like dinosaurs. You know, I believe it is very possible that there may still be dinosaurs in the world, but most of them have probably died out. Maybe there are some in a remote jungle somewhere, just not seen by people. It wouldn't surprise me at all (remember, the average size of a dinosaur was only that of a sheep — and some were as small as chickens), but it would sure surprise evolutionists who say that dinosaurs died out "millions" of years ago.

Isaiah 14:29; Job 41:1, 13–21

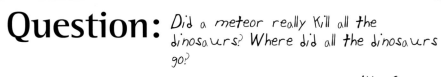

Question:
Did a meteor really kill all the dinosaurs? Where did all the dinosaurs go?

Abby G.

Age 6 — New Mexico, USA

Answer:

Bring out with you every living thing of all flesh that is with you: birds and cattle and every creeping thing that creeps on the earth, so that they may abound on the earth, and be fruitful and multiply on the earth (Genesis 8:17).

The meteor story first started about 1980. Some scientists teach that a huge meteor hit the earth some 65 million years ago and killed all the dinosaurs. Wow! That would be something to see! But I don't believe it happened that way at all. First of all, we know from the Bible that the earth is only about 6,000 years old. Second, why would a meteor strike kill the dinosaurs and leave other animals alive?

So, what did happen to the dinosaurs? Well, Abby, I'll tell you . . . they died! After the Flood, and to this very day, there are many animals that have become extinct (died out) or are on the endangered species list (close to dying out) because of the effects of sin on the earth. Animals become extinct because they are hunted, their land is destroyed, they kill each other, their food supply runs out, or they get diseases that kill them. That is probably exactly what happened to the dinosaurs. It's simple . . . they died!

Genesis 10:9, 8:19

35

DINO CLUB
HUMANS
ALLOWED

Question: Were there people alive when the dinosaurs roamed the earth?

Jim S.

Age 6 — Georgia, USA

Answer:

And God made the beast of the earth according to its kind ... And God saw that it was good. Then God said, "Let Us make man in Our image, according to Our likeness," ... Then God saw everything that He had made, and indeed it was very good. So the evening and the morning were the sixth day (Genesis 1:25, 26, 31).

Dinosaurs and people living together? That is really hard to imagine, isn't it, Jim? Actually, it is not hard to imagine if we are Christians who believe God's Word. Look at our Bible verses. God's Word tells us that dinosaurs (beasts of the earth) and man (Adam and Eve) were actually made on the very same 24-hour day. They were all created on Day 6 of Creation Week. And, it is true that dinosaurs are older than people — but by only a few hours, not millions of years! So, what is the answer to your question? Yes! Dinosaurs lived with people — before the Flood, on Noah's ark with Noah and his family, and after the Flood. God's Word also *describes* what I believe was a dinosaur. In the book of Job, the animal called Behemoth is described, and it sure seems to be a unique, dinosaur-like animal (like a large Sauropod), living right there with Job and the people of that time!

Job 40–41

37

Question: Are dinosaurs related to birds?

Kimberly W.

Age 7 — Georgia, USA

38

Answer:

Then God said, ". . . let birds fly above the earth across the face of the firmament of the heavens." . . . So the evening and the morning were the fifth day (Genesis 1:20, 23).

There are many scientists who believe that dinosaurs evolved into birds. But, if we look at God's Word to find the truth, we'll see that this could not be possible. Why? Because the birds, the flying creatures, were created on Day 5. As you have learned, the dinosaurs were made on Day 6. So, actually, dinosaurs were created *after* birds and could never have turned into birds! Another thing, Kimberly, if you look at a bird and consider a dinosaur, you will see that they are totally different kinds of animals. They have different systems of breathing, they have completely different blood systems, and they have very different bone structures. There are just too many differences between the two. They are unique wonderful creatures created by God. Birds are birds and dinosaurs are dinosaurs and that's it!

Genesis 1:22, 1:28; Romans 1:22–23

Question: How could Noah's children fill the earth?

Josh L.

Age 12 — Pennsylvania, US

40

Answer:

So God blessed Noah and his sons, and said to them: "Be fruitful and multiply, and fill the earth" (Genesis 9:1).

First of all, there are now well over six billion people in the world! I'd say Noah's descendants did a great job of filling the earth. According to the Bible, the Flood was about 4,300 years ago. So, can we account for six billion people starting with only eight just 4,300 years ago? Here is an example for you: Say you get $1.00 on your first birthday. Your parents say they will double your gift on each birthday until you are 21. When you're two you'll get $2, when you're three, you'll get $4, when you're four, you'll get $8, and so on. You just double your birthday gift from the previous year. Well, when you are 21, your gift would be over $1,000,000! Population growth is similar to that. Given enough generations, the number of people being added with each generation would be huge! Just like each of your birthdays above started with more money, each new generation starts with a lot more people. When you do the calculations, you will find that it is very easy to account for six billion people starting with only eight after the Flood.

Genesis 1:28, 9:7

HOLY BIBLE

Question: The books we get from the library state that caves and cave formations took thousands of years to form. We wondered how long they really took and if or how they were related to the world-wide flood.

Adrian & Isaiah W.

Age 10 and 6 — Pennsylvania, U.S.

42

Answer:

They had to live in the clefts of the valleys,
In caves of the earth and the rocks (Job 30:6).

We find cave systems all over our country and the world. I believe most of these cave systems were formed over a short amount of time, not over thousands or millions of years. When we start with the Bible, we see that Noah's flood created conditions that were just perfect for forming all kinds of intricate caves. The water covering the earth left thick layers of limestone and other layers. When the Flood ended, the mountains rose, the valleys sank, and the water flowed off the earth's surface and seeped through the soft sediments. Because water can contain acid dissolved from the air and the soil, this would eat away at the limestone, forming caves. There are also other ways caves can be formed quickly. The dramatic events associated with the flood of Noah's day provided excellent conditions for quick cave formation.

Genesis 8:3, 19:30; 1 Kings 18:13; John 11:38

Question: Why doesn't the Bible tell us about the Ice Age?

Jemima F.

Age 10 — Northern Ireland

44

Answer:

. . . on that day all the fountains of the great deep were broken up, and the windows of heaven were opened (Genesis 7:11).

The Bible is a book of history and altogether true, but God does not reveal everything to us in this book. However, if we look at what we know about the worldwide flood from the Bible, then look at the evidence of glaciers and ice sheets that once covered at least one-third of the earth, we see that the Bible does give us some clues about the Ice Age. A catastrophe as huge as Noah's flood drastically changed the climate on the earth, creating conditions perfect for an Ice Age at the end of the Flood.

The Bible tells us that the fountains of the great deep burst forth. This was unlike anything that we can even imagine! This breaking up of the earth caused the oceans to heat up and caused ash and dust to fill the air, blocking out sunlight, making the temperatures on earth cooler. As the warm water from the oceans evaporated into the air, forming clouds, the colder air over the earth caused wintry conditions, lots of snow, and ice glaciers. This could have very easily caused an Ice Age that lasted hundreds of years. When we start with what the Bible tells us, we can find the truth!

Look at our verse in Job. Maybe this is a reference to the Ice Age at the time of Job.

Job 37:9–10

45

Question:

Since we all came from Adam and Eve, shouldn't we all have the same color of skin?

Emily B.

Age 8 — Alabama, USA

46

Answer:

And He has made from one blood every nation of men to dwell on all the face of the earth, and has determined their preappointed times and the boundaries of their dwellings (Acts 17:26).

For the answer to this question, you'll need a mirror and a white or black piece of paper. Now, if you consider yourself a white, light-colored person, look in the mirror and hold the white piece of paper next to your face. You aren't white at all, are you? If you are a dark-skinned, "black" person, get the black piece of paper, hold it next to your face, and look in the mirror. Are you really black? No! People are some shade of brown, because we all have a brown pigment in our skin called melanin. This is what makes us the shade of color that we are. Some people have a lot of melanin and they would be very dark; some people don't have as much melanin, they would be lighter. I think that Adam and Eve had a medium brown amount of pigment. From such two medium brown people, they would be able to pass on the genes to either produce a really dark child or a really light child. So, Emily, to answer your question, we all do have the same type of skin color . . . it is just that the amount of melanin (brown color) differs from person to person.

Genesis 9:19, 11:9

Answers Are Always Important!

The Bible is truly filled some amazing answers for some of our toughest faith questions. The Answers Book for Kids series answers questions from children around the world in this multi-volume series. Each volume will answer over 20 questions in a friendly and readable style appropriate for children 6–12 years old; and each covers a unique topic, including Creation and the Fall; Dinosaurs and the Flood of Noah; God and the Bible; Sin, Salvation, and the Christian Life; and more!

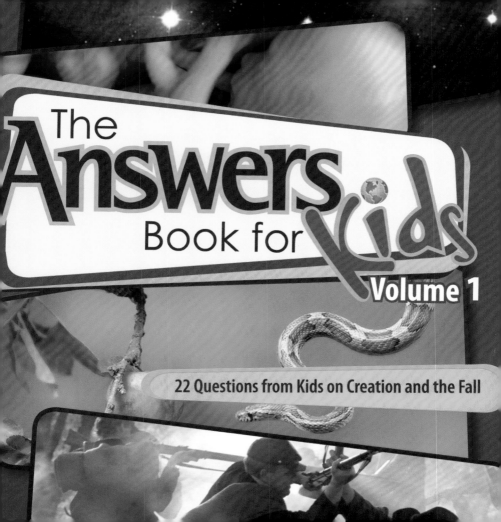

The Answers Book for Kids

Volume 1

22 Questions from Kids on Creation and the Fall

Nineteenth Printing: December 2022

Master Books
P.O. Box 726
Green Forest, AR 72638

Master Books® is a division of the New Leaf Publishing Group, Inc.

Printed in China

Cover Design by Rebekah Krall
Interior Design by Terry White

ISBN 13: 978-0-89051-526-6
SBN 13: 978-1-61458-127-7 (digital)
Library of Congress number: 2008904921

All Scripture references are New King James Version unless otherwise noted.

Please visit our website for other great titles: www.masterbooks.com

When you see this icon, there will be related Scripture references noted for parents to use in answering their children's, and even their own, questions.

For Parents and Teachers

Dear Moms and Dads:

The more I learn about our infinite Creator God, and the longer I serve Him, the more amazed I am at His greatness. As I consider the universe God created, I share David's exclamation in Psalm 145:3, *"Great is the LORD, and greatly to be praised; And His greatness is unsearchable."*

The greatness of God is truly unsearchable when we consider creation. This book is intended to give biblical and scientific answers, in a way children will understand, to questions they have about God's creation and man's fall into sin.

Sadly, our culture today, by and large, has turned away from the truth of God's Word in Genesis. As you know, the Bible makes it very clear that parents are responsible for the teaching of their children. I thank you for allowing me the opportunity to partner with you as we strive to teach children to not only believe God's Word, but to also put their faith and trust in our Savior — the Creator of the universe — Jesus Christ.

Charles Spurgeon once said, "The only way to keep chaff out of the child's cup is to fill it brimful with good wheat." We need to be consistent and intentional as we fill the "cups" of children with the "good wheat" of God's precious, holy Word.

My prayer is that this book will begin to answer many of the questions your children will encounter, but in a way that gives God the glory, honor, and power He is worthy of.

Ken Ham
President/CEO, Answers in Genesis

3

Question: When did time begin?

Sarah S.

Age 10 — Canada

In the beginnin

4

Answer:

In the beginning God created the heavens and the earth (Genesis 1:1).

Time began when God started to create everything in the whole universe. He did this "in the beginning" of the Creation Week. According to the Bible, that was about 6,000 years ago. Before then, there were no days or weeks or years. It is hard for us to understand, but time, just like everything else God created, including you and me, had a beginning, and it wasn't very long ago! God, on the other hand, is infinite. He has always existed, and He is not bound to time, like we are. In fact, the Bible says that to God a day can be like 1,000 years and 1,000 years can be just like a day. Time just doesn't mean the same thing to God as it does to us. He's "outside" of it. We do know, however that He created time on the first day of creation.

2 Peter 3:8; Revelation 1:8

5

Question: How did God create everything from nothing?

Shelby H.

Age 11 — Texas, USA

6

Answer:

By faith we understand that the worlds were framed by the word of God, so that the things which are seen were not made of things which are visible (Hebrews 11:3).

We serve a mighty and powerful God! He created everything — the whole universe — in just six days! And in our Bible verse we learn that the things we see were made from things not seen, or invisible things. In other words, there was nothing (or maybe we should say "not even nothing") when God began to create.

If you read the first chapter of Genesis, you will see the words "God said" eight times. Shelby, this explains how God created by His great power. For example, can you imagine how amazing it must have been when God said, "Let there be lights in the heavens?" The stars, sun, and moon appeared, just as God had planned. God needed only to speak and everything was created. He truly is worthy of our praise!

Exodus 20:11; Genesis 1:14–15

Question:

Did Adam and Eve have bellybuttons?

Kimberly W.

Age 7 — Georgia, USA

8

Answer:

And the LORD God formed man of the dust of the ground . . . and man became a living being. . . . Then the rib which the LORD God had taken from man He made into a woman (Genesis 2:7, 22).

You are not the first one to wonder about Adam's bellybutton! Do you know that our bellybuttons are scars left over from when we were born? When a baby is growing in her mommy's tummy, she needs food. She gets food through a cord attached to her mommy. We all needed that cord in order to survive and grow! Our bellybuttons are scars from the cord that once fed us.

The Bible tells us that our great God made the first man (Adam) directly out of dust. He was already an adult, so he didn't need a cord to get food. The Bible also tells us that God made the first woman (Eve) directly from the rib of the man. So she was an adult too. I think it is very possible they did not have or need bellybuttons.

Genesis 2:4–7, 15–23

Question: Where is the Garden of Eden?

Joy B.

Age 10 — Michigan, USA

10

Answer:

A river watering the garden flowed from Eden; from there it was separated into four headwaters. The name of the first is Pishon. . . . The name of the second river is the Gihon. . . . The name of the third river is the Tigris. . . . And the fourth river is the Euphrates (Genesis 2:10–14 NIV).

Joy, we have absolutely no idea where the Garden of Eden was located. The Bible verse tells us about the Garden of Eden and it even mentions four rivers around the Garden. But there are only two rivers today that have the same names as those where the Garden of Eden was located, the Tigris and the Euphrates; the rest of the description doesn't match. So the Garden of Eden wasn't there.

Also, the worldwide flood of Noah's day would have destroyed everything on the earth, including the Garden of Eden. So why do those two rivers have the same names? Well, I think Noah, or someone in his family, named the rivers. And he used names of rivers that existed before the Flood — names he already knew. Maybe he wanted to be sure that the people would not forget the days before the Flood, and to remind them they must honor and obey God.

Genesis 7:18–23

11

Question: Does Genesis 1:1-2 refer to the first day?

Lee R.

Age 9 — New York, USA

12

Chapter
beginning Go
and the earth
th was w
was

Answer:

So the evening and the morning were the first day (Genesis 1:5).

Yes, Lee, the first two verses of Genesis 1 describe events on the very same day. I presume you ask the question because you have heard that supposedly millions of years passed between verses 1 and 2. You can find the answer to this question if you read closely what Genesis, God's Holy Word, says.

When God first began to create, He created the heavens and the earth. That's verse 1. They weren't completed yet. Verse 2 describes what they looked like so far. The earth was "without form and void" (without life and incomplete). Each day God completed a bit more until, after six days, it was all finished. He called His finished work "very good."

And Lee, you need to know there are many qualified creation scientists who do not believe in millions of years and who have done much scientific research that confirms the universe is only thousands of years old. When you read the Bible carefully, there is no doubt that verses 1 and 2 describe part of the first day.

Genesis 1:1–5

13

Question: When God created the earth, were the trees fully grown, or were they baby trees? If they were full grown, did they have growth rings?

Chris J.

Age 11— California, USA

14

Answer:

And the earth brought forth grass, the herb that yields seed according to its kind, and the tree that yields fruit, whose seed is in itself according to its kind. And God saw that it was good (Genesis 1:12).

Well, let's see. We know by our Bible verse that the trees in the Garden provided fruit for food. And we know that Adam and Eve could eat the fruit from all the trees except one. They didn't need to wait for years for the trees to grow big enough to produce fruit, did they?

It seems that God created the trees to sprout, grow, and bear fruit all in one day. I do believe that the trees had growth rings, for a couple of reasons. First, they were fully grown trees to start with, and most grown trees have growth rings. Second, the growth rings of many trees are actually part of the structure of the tree and support the tree. Some trees would need those growth rings to stand tall and produce fruit for Adam and Eve. So the growth rings were part of what made these trees perfect and very good, like the rest of God's creation.

Genesis 1:29–31

Question: Why did God make a week seven days long?

Caleb F.

Age 6 — Ohio, USA

16

Answer:

For in six days the LORD made the heavens and the earth, the sea, and all that is in them, and rested the seventh day. Therefore the LORD blessed the Sabbath day and hallowed it (Exodus 20:11).

Our Bible verse tells us why God made the week seven days long. Let me explain. He made the seven-day week just for us. He created everything in six days and rested on the seventh day, right? Well, God could have made the entire universe in one split second because He is all-powerful and mighty. But He was setting a pattern for us to follow.

If we just kept on working every single day, we would get very tired and probably get sick. God was showing us that we can work six days, but then we need to rest for one day. Remember that He didn't need to take that long to create everything (and He didn't need to rest). Six days is actually a very long time for God. The seven-day week is for us!

Exodus 16:25–27

17

Question: Why was the first person that God created a boy?

Chloe G.

Age 6 — Illinois, USA

18

Answer:

And the LORD God said, "It is not good that man should be alone; I will make him a helper comparable to him" (Genesis 2:18).

Okay. First of all, this person wasn't exactly a boy. Adam was a man. And we know that, as our infinite Creator, God can do whatever He wants to do. When He made Adam first, God was teaching us how He wanted our families to be. He made Adam to be the head of the family. See in our Bible verse? It says that God wanted to create a "helper" for Adam, so He created Eve. Eve was the perfect complement to Adam.

Adam was the leader of that very first family. Adam was not better or more valuable than Eve. It was just that God knew someone had to be the leader, so He made that leader Adam. By doing this, God showed us that He wants the husband, the dad in the family, to be the spiritual leader in the family.

Ephesians 5:22–25; 1 Corinthians 11:3

Question: Why did God let Adam name the animals? Why didn't He name them himself?

Caleb Z.

Age 11 — Tennessee, USA

Answer:

And the Lord God said, "It is not good that man should be alone; I will make him a helper comparable to him" (Genesis 2:18).

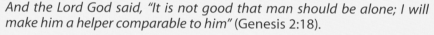

Our Bible verse says that God didn't think it was good for man to be alone. If you keep reading in your Bible, you'll see that the Lord brought animals He had already created to Adam. Now we know that God easily could have named all of those animals. But God was teaching Adam and us a lesson.

You see, as Adam was naming the animals, it became very clear to him that he was completely different from the animals and was a special creation. He was created in God's very image. Keep this in mind, Caleb, when you hear that humans evolved from animals. God's Word tells us just the opposite! Humans are far different from animals, and when Adam understood that he was alone, God put him to sleep to make a "helper" for him, and her name was Eve!

Genesis 2:19–25

21

Question: Did Adam give each of the animals the names we call them today?

Olivia B.

Age 7 — Pennsylvania, USA

22

Answer:

So Adam gave names to all cattle, to the birds of the air, and to every beast of the field (Genesis 2:20).

This question has a couple of answers. Let me explain.

First, Adam didn't name every animal created or each variety and species. He would have only named the "kinds" of animals that God brought to him. (All of the varieties and species would not have been there yet!) In other words, he only named the dog kind, the cat kind, the horse kind, etc.

Second, we don't know what language Adam spoke, so there is really no way of knowing what he called each animal kind. And third, when God later confused all the languages at the Tower of Babel, it is possible that Adam's original language did not survive (if it had survived, we still wouldn't know what it was). As we study the Bible, we see that there is no way of knowing what Adam called the animals. But the names were probably not the same as today. Like for example, the word "dinosaurs." The word wasn't even invented until 1841, but we know from the Bible that these creatures were created along with the other animal kinds. But we do not know the name Adam gave them.

Genesis 11:7–9

23

Question: How long did it take Adam to name the animals?

Sydney C.

Age 8 — Ohio, USA

Answer:

. . .and [God] brought them to Adam to see what he would call them . . . (Genesis 2:19).

Well, a lot of people say there is no way Adam could have had enough time to name all the animals in a single day. Actually, when we read God's Word carefully, we find he didn't name all the animals.

First, we know from Genesis that Adam named only land animals on the sixth day (and he named them before Eve was created on that same day, by the way). This means that he definitely named them within 24 hours, at most!

Second, remember from the previous question that Adam named only "kinds" of land animals and then, only the cattle, birds of the air, and beast of the fields. Adam really named far fewer animals than we think! One more thing — Adam was the most intelligent man that ever lived. God made him with a perfect brain and a perfect memory. It wouldn't take him long to think of the names and to then remember which animal was which! He had plenty of intelligence and plenty of time to name them all in one day!

Genesis 2:18–20

Question: The serpent talked to Eve, so why can't snakes talk today?

Jemimah F.

Age 10 — Northern Ireland

Answer:

So the donkey said to Balaam, "Am I not your donkey on which you have ridden, ever since I became yours, to this day? Was I ever disposed to do this to you?" (Numbers 22:30).

You, Jemimah, are made in God's image, right? You can talk and communicate. You can have a conversation with other human beings (also created in God's image). Animals are not made in the image of God. And yet, you see in our Bible verse that God opened the mouth of a donkey and it talked.

Whenever it will serve God's perfect plan, He can use anything to convey His message, even a donkey.

In the same way, God allowed Satan (the devil) to use the serpent to disguise himself and tempt Eve.

Genesis 3:1–7

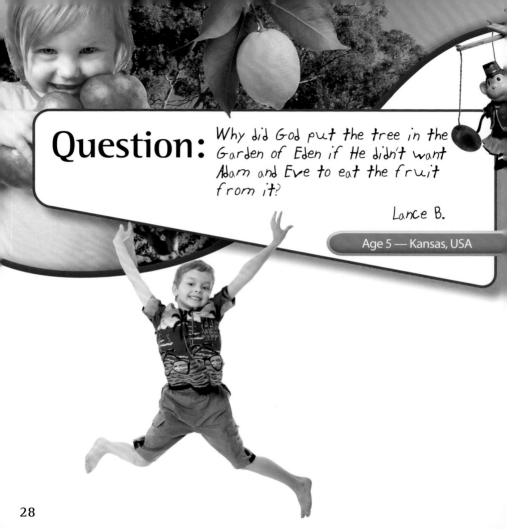

Question: Why did God put the tree in the Garden of Eden if He didn't want Adam and Eve to eat the fruit from it?

Lance B.

Age 5 — Kansas, USA

28

Answer:

. . . but of the tree of the knowledge of good and evil you shall not eat, for in the day that you eat of it you shall surely die (Genesis 2:17).

Have you ever played with a puppet? The puppet will do whatever you want it to do because it is on your hand. You are moving it, talking for it, and making it sit, stand, and dance. Well, when God made Adam, He didn't want him to be a puppet, but He wanted Adam to truly love Him.

The command about the tree of the knowledge of good and evil was God's test to see if Adam really did love God enough to totally obey Him. But Adam failed the test. He sinned against God and did something God told him not to do. This was a very bad day for all of us because Adam was the head of the whole human race — the very first man. When he failed God's test, he brought sin into the world, and now all of us have the same sin nature from Adam.

John 3:16; Romans 5:12

Question: If all that God created was good, how could Satan be bad?

Jordan C.

Age 7 — Indiana, USA

30

Answer:

Then God saw everything that He had made, and indeed it was very good. So the evening and the morning were the sixth day (Genesis 1:31).

The Bible clearly tells us that on Day 6, when God saw all He had made, He called it all "very good." God had to have included the angels with the rest of creation! So Lucifer (or Satan) was very good when God created him. In fact, Lucifer was one of the beautiful angels God had created!

But he soon became proud and wanted to take God's place on His throne. He thought that he could be as great as God. Because God created Adam and Eve as special human beings, Satan wanted them to turn away from God, too. So he told Eve that she could become like God. They believed him, sinned, and were cast out of the Garden.

Isaiah 14:13; James 1:13–15

31

Question: Who was Cain's wife? Why doesn't th Bible mention her birth if she was Eve's baby?

Calista M.

Age 8 — New Hampshire

32

Answer:

After he begot Seth, the days of Adam were eight hundred years; and he had sons and daughters (Genesis 5:4).

Adam and Eve had many children. Adam lived to be 930 years old, and Jewish tradition states that he had 33 sons and 23 daughters. (That is a really big family!)

Most people believe that Cain married his sister or his niece, and the Bible does not tell us what her name was. Keep in mind that way back then (about 6,000 years ago) close relatives could marry — they had to in order to start their own families. Even Abraham married his half-sister. Of course, we can't do that anymore because of the effects of sin on our bodies and because God told Moses that people were not to marry close relatives from that time on. Now when we marry, we marry someone not so closely related to us.

While we're speaking about marriage, Calista, remember that according to God, marriage is one man and one woman until death — that's how God commands it.

Genesis 2:24, 20:12; Leviticus 18:6

Question: Did bumblebees have stingers before Adam and Eve sinned?

Heidi C.

Age 10 — Ohio, USA

34

Answer:

For we know that the whole creation groans and labors with birth pangs together until now (Romans 8:22).

Because of Adam's sin in the Garden, we do not live in a perfect world. We really can't imagine what a perfect world would be like. We know there was no violence and no death — we wouldn't expect this from a loving, life-giving God.

Our Scripture verse tells us that the whole creation is affected by sin, and that includes bumblebees. So, when we consider their stingers, all of us wonder the same thing that you've asked, Heidi. I think it is likely that the bumblebees had what we now call stingers before sin, but they weren't used to harm anything. I am sure they weren't originally meant to sting us, but because of sin in the world, things have changed! When a bumblebee reacts to us in a fallen world, it hurts!

Genesis 3:8–19

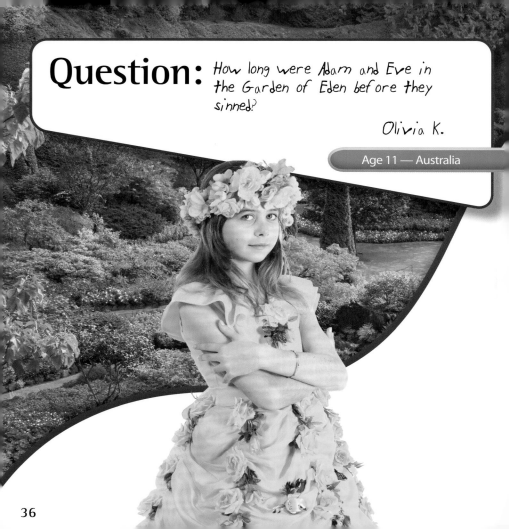

Question: How long were Adam and Eve in the Garden of Eden before they sinned?

Olivia K.

Age 11 — Australia

36

Answer:

Then God blessed them, and God said to them, "Be fruitful and multiply . . ." (Genesis 1:28).

Olivia, let's look at what the Bible says to find an answer. Our verse says that God told Adam and Eve to be fruitful and multiply. In other words, they were supposed to start a family in the Garden. But the Bible also indicates that they had to leave before they had any children.

You see, the Bible tells us that all men are born with the sin of Adam. If Adam and Eve had started their family in the Garden, their children would not have been born in sin or affected by Adam's sin. So, I think they may have been in the Garden only a few days before they sinned and God made them leave.

Romans 3:23, 5:12

37

Question: When were the other planets created?

Joshua C.

Age 8 — Arkansas, USA

Answer:

Then God made two great lights: the greater light to rule the day, and the lesser light to rule the night. He made the stars also. . . . So the evening and the morning were the fourth day (Genesis 1:16, 19).

Our Bible verse tells us that God made the sun, moon, and stars on the fourth day. Although the Bible doesn't specifically say "planets," it is correct to say that the Hebrew word translated "star" included the planets that God spoke into existence on that great day!

God also tells us that He hung these "lights" in the heavens for signs, seasons, days, and years. And another fun fact we find, as we read Genesis 1, is that the earth is actually three days older than all the stars and planets, since the earth was created on Day 1!

Psalm 19:1, 33:6

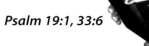

39

Question:

If God created the world 6,000 years ago or so, why are stars millions of light years away?

Brendon M.

Age 10 — Pennsylvania, USA

40

Answer:

The heavens declare the glory of God; and the firmament shows His handiwork (Psalm 19:1).

Brendon, what a question! Yes, we know from the dates God gives us in the Bible that He did create the whole universe about 6,000 years ago. When we hear the term light-year, we need to realize it is not a measure of time but a measure of distance, telling us how far away something is. Distant stars and galaxies might be millions of light-years away, but that doesn't mean that it took millions of years for the light to get here, it just means it is really far away!

When God created the universe, everything was already working perfectly, exactly how He wanted it to work. So, I believe the stars could be seen (however God did that) on earth as soon as God spoke them into existence. Keep enjoying the splendor of the night sky, but remember that God created it to display His glory so we could behold how wonderful and powerful our Creator really is!

Psalm 50:6, 147:4; Isaiah 40:26

41

Question: What is evolution?

Calista J.

Age 8 — New Hampshire, U

42

Answer:

So God created great sea creatures and every living thing that moves, with which the waters abounded, according to their kind, and every winged bird according to its kind. And God saw that it was good (Genesis 1:21).

Calista, the word evolution actually just means "change." Of course, we all know in our world today it usually means something else. When most people hear the word evolution today, they think of Charles Darwin. Darwin believed that one kind of animal evolved into a totally different kind and that eventually ape-like creatures evolved into human beings over millions of years.

This is totally against God's Word, which clearly records that God created all living things according to their kinds (that dogs would only produce dogs, cats only produce cats, and so on). God's Word also states that the first man was made from dust and the first woman from his side (they didn't come from ape-like creatures)! There has never been any scientific evidence to show that one kind of animal (any animal) has ever turned into another totally different kind of animal! God's Word is true.

Romans 1:22; Psalm 8:3–9; Genesis 1:20–25

Question: Why do evolutionists trust their beliefs and not Christ?

Joy B.

Age 11 — Michigan, USA

Answer:

But they deliberately forget that long ago by God's word the heavens existed and the earth was formed out of water and by water (2 Peter 3:5 NIV).

God's Word gives us the answer to your question, Joy. Our Scripture verse says that people "deliberately forget" that God created the universe from nothing, that He spoke it all into existence.

Why don't they believe? Why do they want to forget? We are all born sinners and because of that people just don't want to admit that a powerful, all-knowing God created them. They don't want to admit that God is in control of all things — even them!

They would rather believe that they evolved from slime over millions of years. If this were true, then it means they don't owe God anything. They don't have to obey Him or be grateful for His many gifts. But the Bible makes it very clear that God is our Creator; we are His, and He has a plan for our life. He is the One we need to listen to and obey!

Job 42:2; Ephesians 1:11; Genesis 1:20–25

45

Question: Did God use the same design for humans as for monkeys?

Caleb W.

Age 10 — Missouri, USA

46

Answer:

Then God said, "Let Us make man in Our image, according to Our likeness" (Genesis 1:26).

Have you ever gone shopping and seen a whole bunch of really neat skateboards? You might know what type they are because of how they are painted or designed. They are similar because the same company made them. Well, when you look at God's creation, you find many similarities because the same Maker created them.

God created all living things, and it makes sense that a lot of these share many similar characteristics or design. The same God, the same Designer, created both monkeys and humans and thus there are some similarities. But the differences are also important. Man is not an animal! Our Bible verse here says that man was made in God's image — a monkey wasn't.

Man is very different from a monkey. Man can think, he can appreciate and write music, and he can build airplanes and bridges. Monkeys can't do this. Humans can have a relationship with their God, and we can spend eternity with Him if we believe His Word concerning salvation. We can ask forgiveness for our sins and believe in Jesus Christ, who took the punishment for our sins. Monkeys and animals cannot do that!

Psalm 104; 1 John 3:1; John 1:12

Answers Are Always Important!

The Bible is truly filled some amazing answers for some of our toughest faith questions. The Answers Book for Kids series answers questions from children around the world in this multi-volume series. Each volume will answer over 20 questions in a friendly and readable style appropriate for children 6–12 years old; and each cover a unique topic, including Creation and the Fall; Dinosaurs and the Flood of Noah; God and the Bible; Sin, Salvation, and the Christian Life; and more!

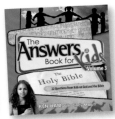

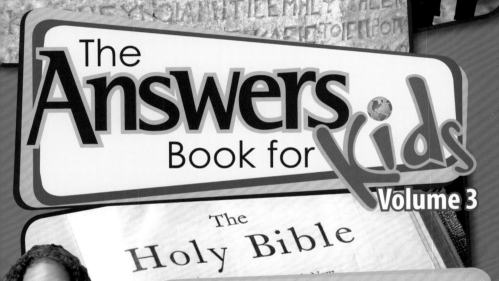

The

Answers

Book for Kids

Volume 3

The

HOLY BIBLE

22 Questions from Kids on God and the Bible

original tongues
former translations diligently
and revised, by His
command

KEN HAM with Cindy Malott

Sixteenth Printing: March 2023

Master Books
P.O. Box 726
Green Forest, AR 72638

Master Books® is a division of the New Leaf Publishing Group, Inc.

Printed in China

Book design by Terry White

ISBN 13: 978-0-89051-525-9
ISBN 13: 978-1-61458-285-4 (digital)

Library of Congress Control Number: 2009900147

All Scripture references are New King James Version unless otherwise noted.

Please visit our website for other great titles: www.masterbooks.com

When you see this icon, there will be related Scripture references
noted for parents to use in answering their children's, and even their
own, questions.

For Parents and Teachers

Therefore whoever hears these sayings of Mine, and does them, I will liken him to a wise man who built his house on the rock: and the rain descended, the floods came, and the winds blew and beat on that house; and it did not fall, for it was founded on the rock (Matthew 7:24-25).

Dear Moms and Dads:

When I think of my father's memorial service and the individual testimonies of each of his six children, I am reminded of the tremendous legacy he left us. In different words and styles, each of us conveyed the same basic theme: Dad always stood up for what he believed, he taught his children to love the Word of God, and he always insisted that the authority of God's Word takes precedence over the fallible words of man. My dad's favorite book was his personal Bible—he loved it. It is well-worn and his study notes appear throughout it.

His words, life, and example demonstrated to me that the only foundation necessary to withstand life's many storms is the knowledge of God through His Word.

You, too, are leaving a legacy to the children in your life. Is your love for the Bible shaping them and the way they look at the world? I pray that this little book will equip you to lead your children to God's Word to find the answers to the questions they have. And that one day, by the power of His Word, they will repent of their sins and claim Jesus Christ as their Lord and Savior. To God be the glory!

Ken Ham
President/CEO, Answers in Genesis

3

Question:

I don't know if I believe in God because, I mean, who made God anyway?

Jason W.

Age 11 — Alabama, USA

4

Answer:

I am the Alpha and the Omega, the Beginning and the End," says the Lord, "who is and who was and who is to come, the Almighty" (Revelation 1:8).

Well, Jason, a lot of very smart people have asked this question. After all, if everything has a beginning or is made out of something or had a creator, then people think God must have had one too! So, let's think about it. If someone made God, then you must have a bigger God who made that God . . . and a bigger, bigger God who made that bigger God who made God. . . then a bigger, bigger, bigger God who made the bigger, bigger God who made the bigger God who made God. You see, Jason, we could go on and on and on. The only thing that makes sense is we have to have the biggest God of all. God—the God of the Bible—is the Creator of everything. Nothing and no one is bigger than Him. He was not created but has always existed. He is the Alpha (beginning) and Omega (end). The Bible says, "In the beginning, God created the heavens and the earth." In the beginning God was already there and He created all things to teach us more about Him and to show us His power, His goodness, and His wisdom.

Genesis 1:1; Psalm 19:1; Revelation 4:11

Question: What does God look like?

Calista M.

6

Answer:

. . . who alone has immortality, dwelling in unapproachable light, whom no man has seen or can see, to whom be honor and everlasting power. Amen (1 Timothy 6:16).

How wonderful it will be to finally see God in all His glory. We read that God lives in light so bright that we could never come near it, and that He is a spirit. When the prophet Ezekiel described his vision of God, he included bright fire, flashes of lightning, even the brightness of a rainbow in a cloud on a rainy day. But we are ALL sinners and the Bible says because of this, we are blind to spiritual things. We are born sinners because of Adam's disobedience in the Garden of Eden. And we can't see God because of our sinfulness. So while we are here on earth, we cannot see Him, we cannot know what He looks like, even though He is present with us. However, we see the glory of God in the face of Jesus Christ as revealed in the Bible. Now there is good news. God loved us and He had a plan that would save us. Jesus Christ stepped into history as a man, died on a cross, and rose from the dead. He promises that everyone who believes in Him, who calls on His name, who is sorry for his or her sins, and receives His free gift of forgiveness and salvation, will one day be with Him in heaven—where we will finally see our holy, merciful God.

*Ezekiel 1; Romans 3:23; John 4:24;
John 3:16; 2 Corinthians 4:6*

HOLY BIBLE

7

Question: Where is God? Why can't I see him?

Rachael S.

Age 6 — Ohio, USA

8

Answer:

But He said, "You cannot see My face; for no man shall see Me, and live" (Exodus 33:20).

We can't see God because He is a spirit—but the Bible says Moses spoke to God face to face! Can we see God like Moses? The Bible tells us He is omnipresent by His Spirit. That means He is everywhere and sees everything all the time. That is very hard to understand, and seems simply amazing, even to me! I get a tiny idea of just how amazing it is when I fly in an airplane (which I do quite a bit). When I go over a big city like Los Angeles or New York and I look down I see thousands and thousands of lights—cars, houses, buildings, shopping malls, lots of people down there. I realize that God sees them at soccer, at the mall, in the house, at church, in the park, playing with their friends, He sees EVERYONE and KNOWS what they are doing! He also knows our hearts. He knows what we are thinking. He knows whether we love Him. He knows our needs. He is everywhere, Rachael, and He knows everything about you. And even though we accept this by faith, it is not a blind faith. You see, what we read in God's Word, which is the primary way God communicates to us today, makes sense of what we see in God's world. Also, in many ways, science confirms God's Word is true. Now God revealed Himself to us in the person of Jesus—when He came to earth as a man. And Rachael, lots of eyewitnesses saw Jesus and the miracles He did! Today we "see Him" through the words of the Bible.

Psalm 139:1-6; John 4:24; 2 Chronicles 16:9

Question: How big is God?

Jemima F.

Age 10 — Northern Ireland

10

Answer:

"...Do I not fill heaven and earth?" says the LORD (Jeremiah 23:24).

We already touched on this in question one, but let's look at it a different way. We tend to think of things in terms of a physical size. For example, we can look at how tall people are, how big the dog is, how high the mountains are, how wide the creek is—you get the idea. We compare the things we see when it comes to size. Some things are very big and some things are very small. But God doesn't have a physical form. Remember? God is spirit and He fills both time and space because He is spirit. We know that God created the universe. (Now that is very big!) And there sure isn't anything in the whole universe we can compare Him to. So, when we talk about how big God is we need to understand that God is infinite. (Infinite means we can't even measure it and there are no words to describe it—it is forever big). He is infinite in power; that's big! He is infinite in wisdom; that's big! He is infinite in knowledge; that's big! I don't think we can begin to imagine just how big He is, but it is fun to think about it.

Genesis 1:1; Nehemiah 9:6;
Jeremiah 10:6; Psalm 86:8

11

Question:

How does God get His power? Where does He get it from?

Miroslava M.

Age 8—Mexico

12

Answer:

Ah, Lord GOD! Behold, You have made the heavens and the earth by Your great power and outstretched arm. There is nothing too hard for You... (Jeremiah 32:17).

We hear a lot about God's power. Take a look at our verse. God's almighty power made the heavens and the earth and there is nothing too hard for God. Well, I want you to learn another big word . . . omnipotent. The Bible clearly teaches that God is omnipotent, meaning He is all powerful. He is Almighty God, He is Lord, the Creator of all things, and He never gets tired! There is none like God. Although we can't completely understand His power, we know He is infinite in power (meaning there is no way to measure it), and all power ultimately comes from Him and the source of His power never becomes exhausted. God can do anything He wants whenever He wants, and nothing is impossible for Him. I am so glad that I serve a God who is all powerful!

Psalm 147:5; Nehemiah 9:6; Mark 10:27

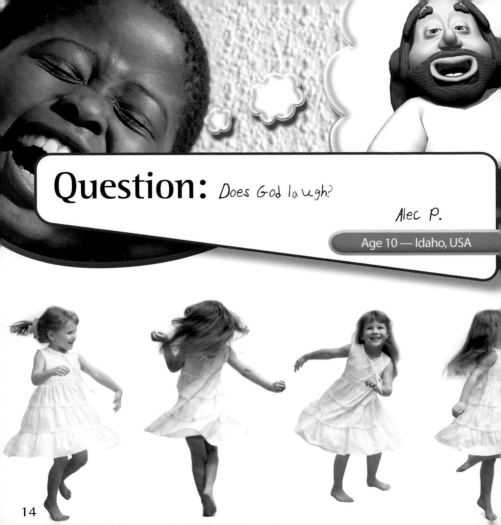

Question: Does God laugh?

Alec P.

Age 10 — Idaho, USA

14

Answer:

The LORD laughs at him, for He sees that his day is coming (Psalm 37:13).

Well, Alec, we were created in God's image, which means that although we don't look like God, we are like God in other ways. God created us to be able to do things that animals can't do. For example, think, write, read, play games, and laugh! I believe that all of the special things we can do as humans reflect a part of who God is. After all, the Bible tells us that God does have emotions. The Bible tells us about times when God was sad (during Noah's day) and when God is happy (when we obey His Word). So yes, God can laugh with joy.

The Bible also tells us about times when God laughs in a different way at foolish people because they think they can do things against Him. They think they can sin, reject God, and ignore His Word. God laughs at these wicked people, not to be mean, but because He knows that in the end He is the only true and perfect God and He will have the last say—and He judges wickedness.

Genesis 1:27; Isaiah 62:5; Psalm 2:4;
Proverbs 1:26; Psalm 16:11

Question: How does God know something before it happens?

Trent C.

Age 11 — Pennsylvania

16

Answer:

But, beloved, do not forget this one thing, that with the Lord one day is as a thousand years, and a thousand years as one day (2 Peter 3:8).

You know, Trent, the Bible tells us that God is outside of time—to Him a day is like a thousand years, and a thousand years are like a day. He therefore knows everything before it happens. He even created time. He is not bound by time and He sees all of life and history from start to finish at the same time! In other words, He sees the end from the beginning. He sees what is past and what is still to come. The Bible confirms this through the prophets (people in the Bible who told about things that hadn't happened yet). God used these people to let others know some of the things that were going to happen. One example is the Prophet Micah who wrote about Jesus being born long before it happened. Today, God still knows exactly what is going on. He is always doing what pleases Him, and what is best for us, AND He knows all things before they happen! He is truly a great and wonderful God, deserving of our worship and praise!

Genesis 1:1; Isaiah 46:9-10;
Micah 5:2-4; Psalm115:3

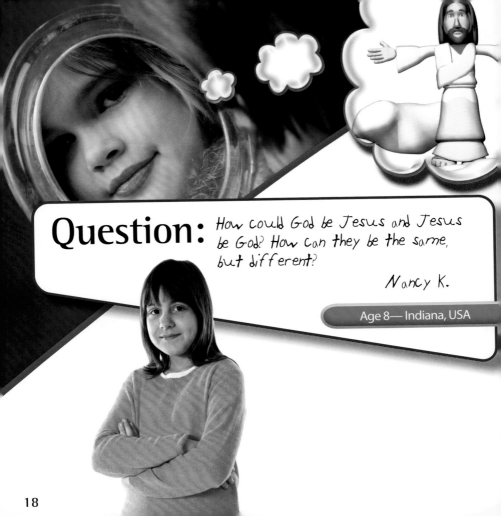

Question: How could God be Jesus and Jesus be God? How can they be the same, but different?

Nancy K.

Age 8— Indiana, USA

18

Answer:

In the beginning was the Word, and the Word was with God, and the Word was God. He was in the beginning with God. All things were made through Him (John 1:1-3).

You are wondering about a very important teaching from the Bible. But there is more here—the Holy Spirit. God is three distinct persons—Father, Son, and Holy Spirit—and each is fully God, yet there is only one God. This is especially hard for us to understand. But remember, God is not like anything else in the whole world.

This might help you to understand a little. In the first chapter of the Bible, God says, "In the beginning God". Now there are some very smart people who study the Bible. These people tell us that the way the word "God" is used here means more than one person. As we read Genesis, we learn that God's Spirit was there at creation, that God Himself spoke all of creation into existence, and Jesus is called the Creator. He is the Creator, and the One who stepped into history and became a man. He did this to help us know God better and to show us how we could one day be with God the Father, God the Son, and God the Holy Spirit. Nancy, because we are created in God's image, we are like Him in some ways—we can think abstractly, love, have relationships and so on. But there are many things very different from us that are hard to understand, and these make God who He is—He is eternal, and He is the triune God. He is one but more than one.

Deuteronomy 6:4; Colossians 1:16; John 1:1

19

Question: Is the Holy Spirit even with God?

Taylor B.

Age 7— Kansas, USA

20

Answer:

"And I will pray the Father, and He will give you another Helper, that He may abide with you forever…" (John 14:16).

Taylor, we assume you are asking is the Holy Spirit equal with God. Well, there is only one God, but there are three persons in one God—the Father, the Son, and the Holy Spirit. Because we are not anything like God, this is a mystery that is very hard to understand. The answer to your question is, yes, the Holy Spirit is even (equal) with God because the Holy Spirit IS God. You see, after Jesus (God the Son) died on the cross, He was buried, and He rose from the dead. He did this so that you could have eternal life with Him if you trust in Him and believe in Him. After Jesus rose from the dead, He did something very special for all of us. See our Bible verse above? It says that Jesus sends a Helper, who comes from the Father, who is the Spirit of truth. Jesus sent this Helper to everyone who believes in Him. This Helper (the Holy Spirit) stays with us. He teaches us to pray. He helps us to understand the Bible. He even helps us to love and help other people (even when they don't love us back!) The Holy Spirit is even with God . . . but He stays with us in our heart so that we have help to obey God even when that seems really, really hard!

John 15:26

Question: Why can't I hear God talking to me?

Alyssa I.

Age 4 — Pennsylvania, USA

Answer:

God, who at various times and in various ways spoke in time past to the fathers by the prophets, has in these last days spoken to us by His Son ... (Hebrews 1:1-2).

So, Alyssa, you can't actually "hear" God, right? Well, our verse tells us that long ago, before the Bible was ever printed, God did speak to people. He spoke so they would know what He wanted and so they would know Him. He only spoke to those people He chose and they shared God's words with the others. But you see, those people way back then did not have the Bible, God's written word. We are so blessed to have God's Word. It is like a long letter from God. This letter is like other letters you might get from your mom, grandma, or a friend. When you read a letter, you know that someone is "talking" to you, don't you? It is the same with the Bible. We don't need to hear God out loud because we can "hear" what He has to say by reading the Bible. We think it might be easier if God would just speak out loud and then we would know what He wanted. But He promises that if we study His word we will get to know Him. We need to read it and study it. We need to trust it. When we do that, we WILL hear God through His Word!

2 Timothy 3:16-17; Proverbs 30:5-6

Question:

How do we know that God really answers prayers? Couldn't it be just a coincidence?

McKenzie D.

Age 8 —Tennessee, USA

24

Answer:

But you, when you pray, go into your room, and when you have shut your door, pray to your Father who is in the secret place; and your Father who sees in secret will reward you openly (Matthew 6:6).

First of all, there are no coincidences with God because He always works all things together according to His plan. He is in charge of everything and His plans always work out. God does answer prayers—and He wants us to pray. He told us to pray and He told us how to pray. I don't believe He would do that if He wasn't going to listen and answer! Jesus Himself prayed to God the Father a lot while He was on earth. Remember that God doesn't always answer prayer the way we think He should. There are times when we see a wonderful answer to prayer really quickly. Then there are times when it might take years of praying before God answers. There are also times when we may never see God's answer to a special prayer. And we need to understand that sin affects our prayers. Sometimes without realizing it or being willing to admit it we pray selfishly for things we shouldn't! We need to continually pray the Lord will show us His Will for our lives. He wants us to pray, He wants us to praise Him in our prayers, and He wants us to ask Him to meet our needs. Praying is talking to God as though He were a very good friend . . . He likes hearing from you that way, so keep it up—He will answer! But He will always answer in the way that He knows is best for us.

Romans 8:28; Job 42:2;
Mark 1:35; Hebrews 11:6

25

Question: Why did God create sin?

Eddy R.

Age 11 — New Hampshire, U

OK, I ADMIT IT.. HE DID IT!

26

Answer:

Therefore, just as through one man sin entered the world, and death through sin, and thus death spread to all men, because all sinned (Romans 5:12).

Sin is an action or thought that is in disobedience to God. God created all the heavens and all the earth. He created birds, dinosaurs, the oceans, the earth, the stars, everything including you and me and all people! But He did NOT create sin. When God created people, He knew we would disobey Him—though He created Adam and Eve with the potential to sin. And when Adam and Eve sinned (disobeyed God) in the Garden, the Bible tells us that in Adam the whole human race sinned and fell. Now this is the really amazing part! God uses our sin to show how loving, just, and merciful He is to us. You see, it is because of our sin that God stepped into history to be a man—Jesus—to die on the cross, to be raised from the dead, and to be saved from the punishment for sin. God shows us how much He loves us by forgiving our sins and giving us a way to get to heaven. If we believe in Him and trust Him as Lord of our lives, we will go to heaven because Jesus took the punishment for our sin. So, we are to blame for sin not God. But because of our sin, God wants to save us and show us the most amazing love He has for us. He is a wonderful God!

Romans 3:23; Romans 6:23; John 3:16

Question:

In the Bible God is a God of second chances. God gives us a second chance when we sin. So, why didn't God give Adam and Eve a second chance in the Garden of Eden even though they sinned?

Corey C.

Age 11 — Michigan, USA

28

Answer:

For by grace you have been saved through faith, and that not of yourselves; it is the gift of God, not of works, lest anyone should boast (Ephesians 2:8-9).

We should be careful when using the word "chance," since it can mean something just happened by accident. From God's perspective, nothing happens by "chance" because He knows everything. However, chance can also mean "opportunity," which seems to be how you used it. In one sense, God did give Adam and Eve a second chance because He did not immediately eliminate them for their sin, which is what they deserved. When they sinned, the whole creation fell—it was no longer perfect, and nothing could change that. Adam and Eve were sent out of the Garden so they could not eat from the tree of life and live forever. Can you imagine how dreadful it would be to live in a sin-cursed world for eternity? When God killed that very first animal and clothed Adam and Eve, He shared a picture of the gospel with them. He helped them understand that a perfect sacrifice would be required to take away the sins of all people. That perfect sacrifice would be God Himself—Jesus Christ. Everyone who believes in Jesus Christ as Lord and Savior will receive the free gift of eternal life. God gave us something far better than a "second chance." He offers us a free gift—forgiveness through Jesus, which we can receive by turning from our sin and trusting in Jesus Christ.

Genesis 2:16–17, 3:22–23; Acts 4:12

HOLY BIBLE

29

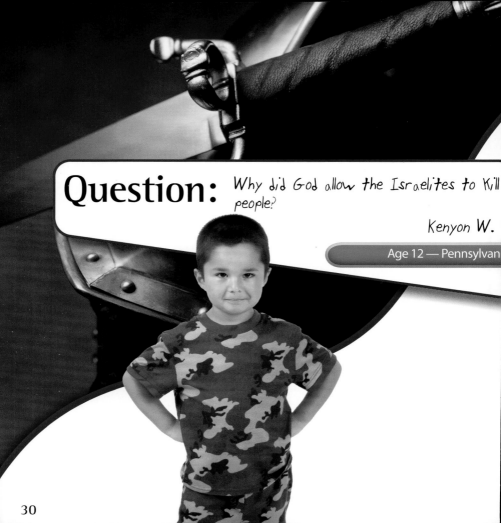

Question:
Why did God allow the Israelites to Kill people?

Kenyon W.

Age 12 — Pennsylvan

30

Answer:

Then the LORD saw that the wickedness of man was great in the earth, and that every intent of the thoughts of his heart was only evil continually (Genesis 6:5).

Our verse from Genesis tells us two very important things—that people of the earth were wicked and that God knows all the thoughts and intents of man's heart. It seems like the Israelites killed innocent people. But we need to learn a couple of things here. First, there are no innocent people . . . the Bible clearly says that we ALL have sinned against a holy and just God. Second, God did not only allow the Israelites to kill the people, He commanded them to do it. Because God is holy, He needs to judge sin and wickedness. He used the Israelites to judge the people and remove the evil in the land. We know there are still evil, wicked people today. But God doesn't command us to destroy those people in the same way. That is because Jesus Christ died on the cross. God judged the sin in the world by punishing His Son on the cross. The Bible tells us that God Himself will judge those who do not claim Jesus Christ as their Savior--those who do not receive Jesus' free gift of forgiveness and who refuse to trust Him and believe in Him as the one and only way to heaven.

Deuteronomy 9:1-4; Psalm 14:2-3;
2 Peter 3:7; Romans 10:13

Question: Why did God create us?

Joy B.

Age 11 — Michigan, US

32

Answer:

For of Him and through Him and to Him [are] all things, to whom [be] glory forever. Amen. (Romans 11:36).

Many, many people, young and old, have asked similar questions. What is my purpose? Why did God create me? The answer is very simple and very clear in the Bible. God created us to glorify Him and to enjoy Him forever. We were created by Him and for Him. He did not need us because He was lonely or wanted someone to talk to. God is perfect and complete and has always been that way. We belong completely to Him. Because of that, we are to glorify Him in everything that we do. How do we do that? We love Him, obey Him, believe in Jesus Christ, trust in Jesus, receiving the free gift Jesus offers us . . . only then will we give glory to God, and only then we will be able to enjoy Him forever, for all eternity!

*Zephaniah 3:17; 1 Corinthians 10:31;
1 Peter 4:11*

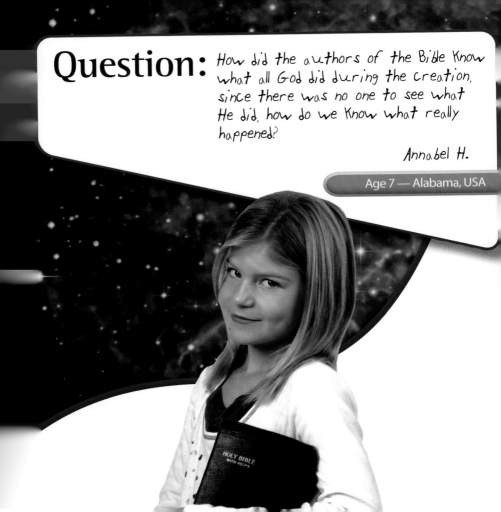

Question: How did the authors of the Bible know what all God did during the creation, since there was no one to see what He did, how do we know what really happened?

Annabel H.

Age 7 — Alabama, USA

Answer:

God is not a man, that He should lie . . .(Numbers 23:19).

Let's see, Annabel. There are people who believe in evolution who think that billions of years ago (when no one was there to see) the universe came into existence by a big bang. Then billions of years ago (when no one was there to see) the earth came into existence. Then billions of years ago (when no one was there to see) life formed on earth. Then millions of years ago (still no one there to see!) animals began changing into other animals. Then two million years ago (yep, still no one there!) an animal like an ape began to change into a human being. That's their story . . . but there wasn't anyone around to see it. Well, guess what? In the Bible we are told that God has given His word to men to write down so we can know how everything came to be. The Bible, which is God's Word, though penned by man, tells us that God WAS there and He has given us an eyewitness account of exactly how the universe and everything in it was created. The Bible tells us thousands of times that it is the Word of God. My questions to you is, "Do you trust God, who knows everything, who has always been there, who never changes, and who doesn't tell a lie OR a human being who doesn't know everything, changes his mind, changes his story, and wasn't always there?" Well, I believe God and that makes real sense!

Malachi 3:6; Luke 21:33;
Genesis 1:1

HOLY
BIBLE

35

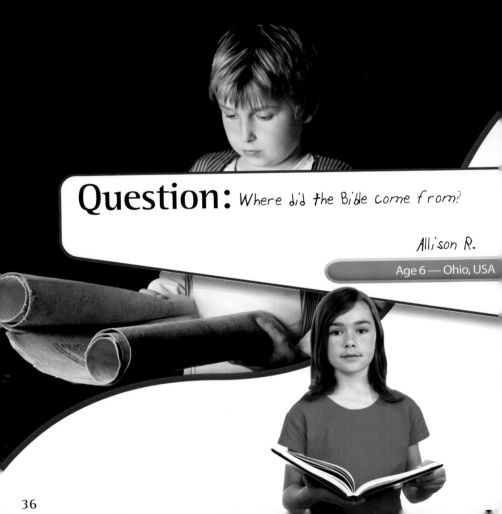

Question: Where did the Bible come from?

Allison R.

Age 6 — Ohio, USA

36

Answer:

. . . for prophecy never came by the will of man, but holy men of God spoke as they were moved by the Holy Spirit (2 Peter 1:21).

Look at our verse above. It says that the Bible came from holy men of God. These men were inspired by God through the Holy Spirit working in their hearts. There were about 40 different writers over a very long time who wrote the Bible. They were from many different life styles—like a doctor, a farmer, and even a fisherman. Just like there were different people, there are different types of writing, like history, poetry, and prophecy (which tells about the future). The amazing thing about the Bible is that even though so many people wrote it over such a long time, it has just one message, it tells one story, and it points to one person, Jesus Christ our Lord and Savior. There is no other book like it on this earth. And if you are called by God, His words will be the joy and the delight of your heart!

*2 Timothy 3:16; Psalm 119:89;
Proverbs 30:5-6; Matthew 4:4*

Question: How did God communicate with Moses?

Krystianna L.

Age 8 — California, USA

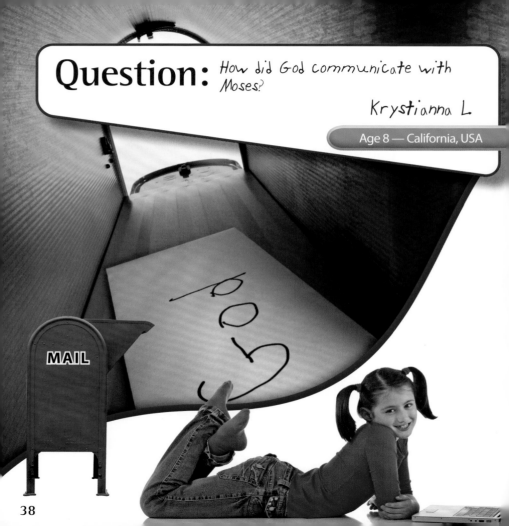

MAIL

Answer:

So the LORD spoke to Moses face to face, as a man speaks to his friend. . . . (Exodus 33:11).

Can you imagine it? Speaking to God? Look at our verse. It says that the LORD spoke to Moses as a man speaks to his friend. How wonderful that must have been. Actually, the Bible tells us that God spoke out loud to Moses many times as he led the Israelites to the Promised Land. God wanted to be sure the people knew exactly what He expected of them. It must have been incredible for Moses because we read in Exodus that after God spoke to Moses his face would shine bright. I believe that the Bible's account of God speaking to Moses is one of the many wonderful, miraculous things we read about in the Bible. The shining face of Moses also reminds us of how holy God is!

Exodus 33:20-23; Exodus 3:4;
Exodus 19:19

39

Question: Just why is the Bible true? I believe but I just don't understand why it's true.

Bennett F.

Answer:

All Scripture is given by inspiration of God, and is profitable for doctrine, for reproof, for correction, for instruction in righteousness… (2 Timothy 3:16).

The Bible is no ordinary book for many reasons. Paul in his letter to Timothy tells us that the Bible Is God's "inspired" Word. In fact, in the original Greek language of the New Testament, the word "inspired" really means that the words of the Bible have been "breathed out" by God through the men who wrote them down. If the Bible is from God, we would expect it to be true and we should be able to test it. We can do this in many ways. In Genesis chapters 1 – 11 we can read an account of many historical events concerning the beginning of this world. Through application of science we can confirm that God's account of creation is true. As an example, God tells us in Genesis chapter 1 that animals, plants, birds, fish, and every living thing were created after their own kind (dogs only produce dogs, etc.). This is exactly what we observe. We are also able to confirm many other aspects of the Bible's history in other areas of science such as geology and astronomy. We can also rely on the Bible's truth concerning Jesus—for instance, in considering how many prophecies about Him were made hundreds of years before He came to earth as a man. Because we can confirm the history in the Bible, we can have faith in all that the Bible has to say. However, the main reason we can trust the Bible is because it is from God—which is different from every other book on earth. Thus we should use the Bible as the starting point for all our living, learning, and actions.

2 Corinthians 5:17; 2 Peter 1:20, 21;
Colossians 1:16-17; John 14:6

Question: Why is it that whenever I mention anything about the Bible in school I get into trouble?.

Carynn B.

Age 9 — Illinois, USA

42

Answer:

I have given them Your word; and the world has hated them because they are not of the world, just as I am not of the world (John 17:14).

Jesus gave us His Word and He told us that the world would hate us because of it. If you are a Christian, you are different from the rest of the world. It is a very sad situation here in America that in public schools there is much confusion about God and the Bible, and what people can say or do. Many want to keep "religion" completely out of the schools. But when we try to keep God out of schools we end up teaching the kids that there is no God. They are learning that the universe can be explained without God. Well, that IS a religion. It is the religion of atheism, believing in NO god. I believe that people are afraid of God's Word and they don't want to have anything to do with it. Why? Because to believe God's Word means you allow Him to make all the rules. It means He tells us that we are sinners and He has the right to tell us what is right and wrong. People just don't like being told they are sinners in rebellion against God, and they don't like being told what to do. The Bible warns us that we will be treated badly because we believe in Jesus. We need to know what the Bible says and share it with others so they can see that it is actually a wonderful book, a book of truth that shows us the way to eternal life by believing and trusting in Jesus.

Matthew 12:30; James 4:4;
Romans 8:7; Romans 10:9

43

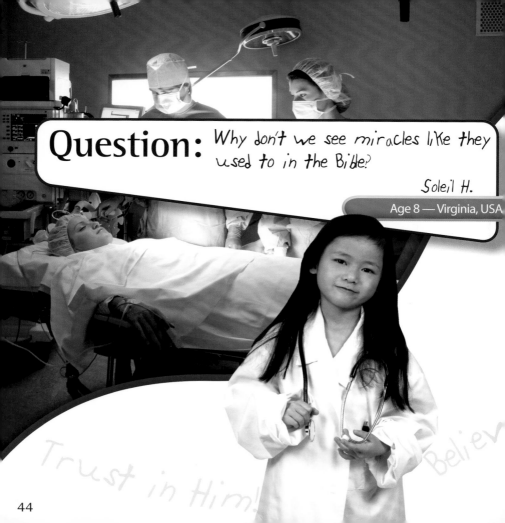

Question: Why don't we see miracles like they used to in the Bible?

Soleil H.

Age 8 — Virginia, USA

Trust in Him!

Believe

44

Answer:

Now these things [such as the miracle of the crossing of the Red Sea] happened to them as an example, and they were written for our instruction… (1 Corinthians 10:11).

Miracles are very special events performed by the power of our almighty, holy God. We read about many miracles in the Bible. In the Old Testament, God used miracles to show the people that He was the ONE true God! He parted the Red Sea, brought terrible plagues, fed the Israelites in the wilderness. In the New Testament, Jesus did miracles as signs so people would know He was the Son of God as He claimed. He walked on water, healed the sick, and even raised the dead! We don't need such signs today as we have God's Word, the Bible. However, God is still a God of miracles today. We all pray for healing from sickness from time to time, either for ourselves or for others. God may or may not give physical healing at that time. The prayer of faith always includes a "but if not" (Dan. 3:18). God changing our hearts from desiring evil to desiring Him IS a wonderful miracle I pray has occurred in your life. God is pleased with our faith as we put our trust in His Word and the miracles written there, given to us as examples to learn about who God is and to obey Him. And when we look at the creation, we are seeing the miracle of life every day! Don't forget, the greatest miracle ever is that God Himself stepped into history as a man, Jesus Christ, and He died, was buried, and rose again! That's the miracle we all need to believe in.

Exodus 7:5; John 11:42;
1 Corinthians 15:3-4

45

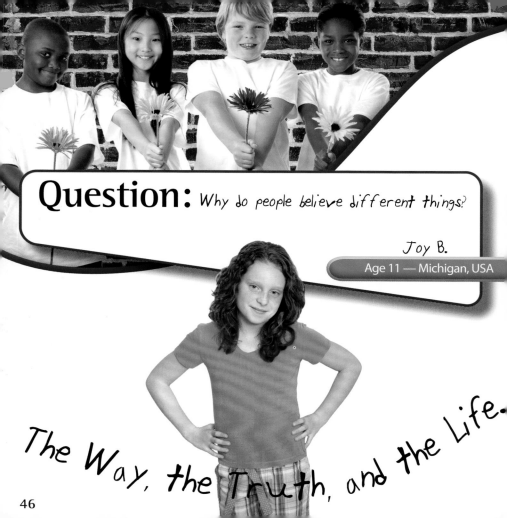

Question: Why do people believe different things?

Joy B.
Age 11 — Michigan, USA

The Way, the Truth, and the Life.

46

Answer:

… who suppress the truth in unrighteousness… (Romans 1:18).

Well, think about it. It was 6000 years ago when the first person decided to believe a truth different from God's. It was in the Garden of Eden—Adam and Eve believed Satan instead of God and they ate the forbidden fruit. When they disobeyed God, they showed us that they wanted to decide their own truth. Since then, men have sinned by ignoring God's truth and believing different things. Our Bible verse tells us they 'suppress the truth'—their heart does not want the true God. People believe so many different things because they are sinners and they don't want to listen to God. The Bible tells us clearly that we must believe God's Word. It tells us that if we don't believe God's Word we will spend eternity separated from Him. My prayer is that you will come to believe the one truth that can save you by putting your faith and trust in the Lord Jesus who is the only way to God the Father and heaven. And you can be sure that if you have any questions about God, Jesus, or how to get to heaven, the Bible will give the answer. It is the true Word of God!

Genesis 3:4-7; Jeremiah 17:9;
John 5:24

HOLY BIBLE

47

Answers Are Always Important!

The Bible is truly filled some amazing answers for some of our toughest faith questions. The Answers Book for Kids series answers questions from children around the world in this multi-volume series. Each volume will answer over 20 questions in a friendly and readable style appropriate for children 6–12 years old; and each covers a unique topic, including Creation and the Fall; Dinosaurs and the Flood of Noah; God and the Bible; Sin, Salvation, and the Christian Life; and more!

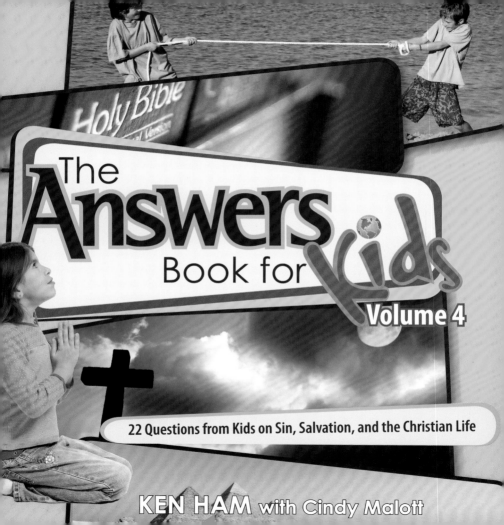

The
Answers
Book for Kids

Volume 4

22 Questions from Kids on Sin, Salvation, and the Christian Life

KEN HAM with Cindy Malott

Fifteenth Printing: August 2022

Master Books
P.O. Box 726
Green Forest, AR 72638

Master Books® is a division of the New Leaf Publishing Group, Inc.

Printed in China

Cover and interior design by Terry White

ISBN 13: 978-0-89051-528-0
ISBN 13: 978-1-61458-081-2 (digital)
Library of Congress Control Number: 2009900146

All Scripture references are New King James Version unless otherwise noted.

Please visit our website for other great titles: www.masterbooks.com

When you see this icon, there will be related Scripture references noted for parents to use in answering their children's, and even their own, questions.

For Parents and Teachers

The fear of the LORD is the beginning of wisdom; and the knowledge of the Holy One is understanding (Proverbs 9:10).

Dear Moms and Dads:

Let's face it. Some questions are just more difficult to answer than others. Did Satan sin first? Why do animals die when they don't sin? Why do I get sick? Did God create the tsunami? What is heaven like? Did God create sin? Questions like these asked by our children today can leave us stumped.

It seems that after decades of studying the Bible, the more I know, the less I know! How can a book be so deep and rich in new wisdom and knowledge? It is a wonderful, blessed mystery that because His works are so great and His thoughts are so deep we will continue to learn about Him throughout all eternity (Psalm 92:5).

As we train up the children in our lives in the way they should go, we must remember to set the example of seeking answers in God's Word—even for the toughest of questions.

I pray that all the children who will be influenced by this book, will one day turn to the Bible to find the most important answer—the life-giving answer—that eternal life comes through belief, trust, and faith in Jesus Christ alone.

Ken Ham
President/CEO, Answers in Genesis

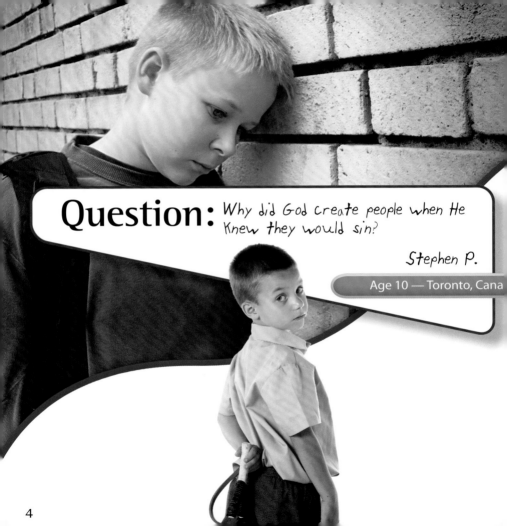

Question: Why did God create people when He knew they would sin?

Stephen P.

Age 10 — Toronto, Cana

Answer:

Oh, the depth of the riches both of the wisdom and knowledge of God! How unsearchable are His judgments and His ways past finding out! (Romans 11:33).

All things have been created by God to give Him glory. God is perfect and has complete knowledge of things past, present, and future. Everything He does is perfect. So, Stephen, how do I answer your question? Well, because we know God is perfect, we know that the entrance of sin into the world through Adam and Eve must have been a way to bring glory to God. But how could sin bring God glory? God is holy, hates sin, and the punishment for sin is death. Well, God had the wonderful plan to save sinners from eternal death through Jesus Christ. Jesus took the punishment for the sins of everyone who would believe in Him even though He had never committed a single sin. Jesus' amazing life, death, and Resurrection shows us how great God's love is for us. When we realize all that Jesus did so we could be saved, we want to shout for joy and give God all the glory! By creating Adam and Eve, God created beings to whom He could show His attributes — love, mercy, and so on. And think about it — by doing this, He has enabled us to exist and to be able to spend forever with our Creator!

Romans 11:36

Question: Could God forgive our sins without the suffering of Christ?

Cheyenne

Age 9 — Belgium

6

Answer:

Nor is there salvation in any other: for there is no other name under heaven given among men, by which we must be saved (Acts 4:12).

Cheyenne, when we sin — when anyone sins — we are telling God, our Creator, that we don't want to obey Him anymore. Well, because He is our Creator, because He is holy and good, He must punish us when we sin. The punishment for sin is serious — eternal death and separation from God forever — unless we could offer a perfect sacrifice to God to pay for our sin. But we are NOT perfect. So, what do we do? Well, God had a plan. And it is a plan that provides a PERFECT sacrifice for you and me! That sacrifice was the Son of God; Jesus Christ. Jesus never did one single sin. He never lied, stole anything, or disobeyed His mother. In fact, He is the only person in the whole world who ever lived and did not sin! But He is the one who had to die for our sins. Our sin against God is so bad that it could only be paid for by Jesus Christ (the perfect One) suffering and dying in our place. Because of our sin in Adam, suffering was the consequence and in one man, Jesus, the full consequence was taken on our behalf. Jesus paid the price for our sin in full. Therefore, He suffered so that He could defeat suffering for all eternity for all who will believe.

When we trust Jesus and believe in Him, we can know that our sins are forgiven because Jesus Christ suffered for us and paid sin's penalty.

2 Corinthians 5:21; Romans 5:8

Question: Will God and Jesus keep me safe from Satan's fallen angels?

Nathan D.

Age 5 — Kentucky, USA

8

Answer:

For I am persuaded that neither death nor life, nor angels nor principalities nor powers, nor things present nor things to come, nor height nor depth, nor any other created thing, shall be able to separate us from the love of God which is in Christ Jesus our Lord (Romans 8:38–39).

It does seem like Satan and his angels might be able to do us harm, doesn't it, Nathan? And the Bible says that the devil prowls around like a roaring lion looking for us! We are told to flee from the devil — and we should do that when we know we are being tempted to do wrong things. Also, God promises His children, those who believe and trust in Jesus and live for Him, that He will never leave us. God's Word makes it clear in Romans 8 that when we trust in Christ, He is with us for eternity and no one can take that away from us. He is our helper and we should not fear! Sometimes, even though you know all of this is true, you still wonder, "What can I do when I still don't feel safe?" Well, bad things still happen on this earth, and God knew we might feel unsafe and scared. The Bible helps us with this, too! It tells us we must be prepared. We must put on the armor of God! No, it is not real metal armor, but something even better! It is the truth of His Word. Reading the Bible and having faith that what it says is true will keep us prepared for anything that happens here on earth. Because we will know that as His children, nothing will ever separate us from His love and one day we will spend all of eternity with Him in a perfect world.

1 Peter 5:8; Hebrews 13:5-6; Ephesians 6:10-18

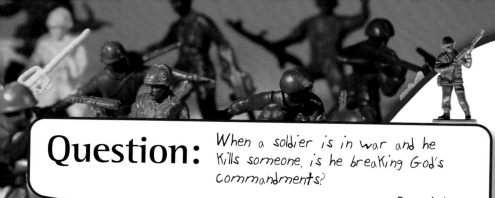

Question: When a soldier is in war and he kills someone, is he breaking God's commandments?

Sam W.

Age 8 — Texas, USA

Answer:

You shall not murder (Exodus 20:13).

Well, Sam, I think we need to take a very close look at God's commandment. See our verse? It actually says that we should not "murder." What the Bible teaches is that we should never kill another person (or even have hatred in our heart) because we're mad at them or jealous or just don't like them. Do you remember the very first murder? When Cain killed Abel? God knew that Cain was jealous of Abel, and that's why he killed him. We see in the Bible where God often instructed the Israelites to go to war in order to accomplish His purpose. Because of the sinfulness of man, God told the Israelites they had to fight against these rebellious people. This was a time of war — and very different from when there is hateful intention by someone and they take things into their own hands and kill (murder) someone. It is sad but true that as long as there is sin in the world, there will always be war. But keep in mind, when a soldier goes to war it is not "murder" because he is obeying his orders and defending himself against the enemy. He is not doing it to be hateful and he would stop fighting if the war was over.

Genesis 4:3-8; 1 Samuel 15:3

Question: When we go to heaven, we have to be perfect up there or wherever. Doesn't that mean our personalities will be changed and everyone will be the same?

Jaden W.

Age 12—North Dakota, US

12

Answer:

And God will wipe away every tear from their eyes; there shall be no more death, nor sorrow, nor crying. There shall be no more pain, for the former things have passed away (Revelation 21:4).

Everyone will NOT be the same in heaven! We will be ourselves without sin! In other words, Jaden, you will never want to lie again . . . you will never have to worry about stuff being stolen . . . you will never be disobedient or selfish. But I believe each person will still be different from all the other people. I believe we will be different because when I look around the world and universe I see that our Creator (God!) LOVES variety. There are so many different, wonderful creatures, plants, stars, galaxies, and unique people. Also, there is a specific example in the Bible that helps answer your question. There was a time when Jesus went up a mountain with his friends, Peter, James, and John. While they were there, they saw Moses and the prophet Elijah . . . and they recognized them! That tells me that they must have looked different from each other — that Moses was still Moses and Elijah was still Elijah. And when Jesus showed Himself to people after He rose from the dead, He had a body, His disciples eventually recognized Him, but He was the same perfect Jesus. In heaven we will be individual people . . . that don't sin! It will be wonderful.

1 Corinthians 13:12; 1 John 3:2

13

Question:
Why does God let the bad guys win sometimes?

Samuel P.

Age 9 — California, USA

Answer:

For indeed I am raising up the Chaldeans,
A bitter and hasty nation
Which marches through the breadth of the earth,
To possess dwelling places that are not theirs (Habakkuk 1: 6).

First of all, let's remember that when God created the universe it was all "very good." Bad things started happening when sin entered the world — after Adam chose to rebel and disobey God. Having said that, we need to also remember that God is all-powerful and all-knowing. Nothing surprises Him! He can do all things and no plan of His can be stopped! Look at our Bible verse above. In this instance, God used the bad guys (the Chaldeans). He ordered them to move, and He allowed them to win! It seems like a bad thing — but God NEVER does anything bad. God had a purpose then for the Israelites and the Chaldeans that would bring Him glory in the end. We can't see all that God sees. God knows exactly how everything will turn out. And in the end, God will judge all the "bad guys" (just as He eventually judged the Chaldeans), even though, from our limited human perspective, it seems they often win. In fact, the Bible says that we are all "bad guys" because we all sin against Him. And unless we are sorry for our "bad-guy ways" (sin) and trust and believe in Jesus Christ as our Savior, we too will face God's punishment.

Psalm 94:1-3; 1 Corinthians 15:24-25

15

Question: Why isn't Satan the first sinner instead of Adam and Eve?

Ben F.

Age 7 — California, USA

16

Answer:

Therefore, just as through one man sin entered the world, and death through sin, and thus death spread to all men, because all sinned (Romans 5:12).

Sin actually entered the world through one man — Adam. Adam was God's special creation, the very first man. When Adam was created on day six, God said that he was to rule over all the earth and all that was on it. God also clearly told Adam not to eat of the fruit of the tree and if he ate he would surely die. Adam was the one who was given the instruction to obey what God said. So, because Adam was told to obey, and Adam chose to disobey God and eat the fruit, and Adam was given dominion to rule over the earth, Adam gets the blame for sin. Sin entered the world — to all of us — through Adam because we are his descendants. So, what about Satan? He was not the father of the human race (it was Adam), he had not been given dominion over all the earth (that was Adam, too), and so he is not the one responsible for sin in our world today. Adam's sin is considered the first sin . . . his is the sin that brought judgment on the human race and, in fact, on the entire creation. It is also important to understand that there is no way for Satan or fallen angels to have salvation. They have already been judged and thrown from heaven. Humans can have their sins forgiven. Therefore, the way God deals with humans is different from the way He deals with the angels.

Genesis 1:26; Genesis 2:16-17; Romans 8:22

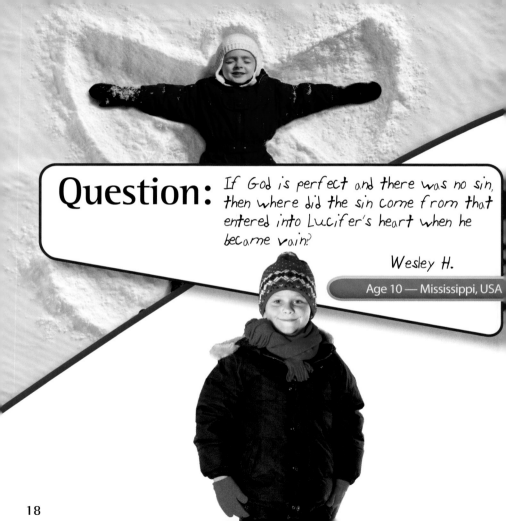

Question: If God is perfect and there was no sin, then where did the sin come from that entered into Lucifer's heart when he became vain?

Wesley H.

Age 10 — Mississippi, USA

18

Answer:

For by Him all things were created that are in heaven and that are on earth, visible and invisible, whether thrones or dominions or principalities or powers. All things were created through Him and for Him (Colossians 1:16).

God is perfect — we know that! Your question, Wesley, talks about Lucifer's sin and Lucifer's heart. This is where we need to be careful. Yes, the Bible tells us some things about Lucifer (Satan) and angels . . . but it is not a book about angels. God tells us in His Word that angels are created beings; they can never be like God. They are not all-powerful or all-knowing. Because they are not all-powerful, they can choose evil. Lucifer chose to turn away from God and became evil. He wanted Adam and Eve to turn away from God by disobeying Him, and Satan is still trying to get people to turn away from God today.

I believe that the sin and vanity in Lucifer's heart came when he chose evil over good and stopped glorifying the One who created him, the One who is all good and holy. Lucifer's rebellion was his own choice to turn against God. Because Adam listened to Satan instead of God, sin was brought into the creation. And please remember that although the Bible does tell us a little about angels, it is really a book about God and His wonderful plan to save people (like you and me) through Jesus Christ.

Jude 6; Genesis 3:1; John 17:3

19

Question: Why do animals die? We are the ones who sinned, so why are they punished? They didn't do anything wrong.

Samantha L.

Age 10 — Pennsylvania, USA

PRESIDIO OF SAN FRANCISCO
PET CEMETERY

GYPSY
1962 — 1976
THE CAT WHO

20

Answer:

For we know that the whole creation groans and labors with birth pangs together until now (Romans 8:22).

It is so very sad when an animal dies — especially a favorite pet. And you are right; they don't sin because they have no souls. But the Bible says that all things will die on earth because of Adam's sin in the Garden of Eden. Let me explain. If the principal at your school said there would be no recess, it affects everyone at your school because he is the head of your school, right? Well, God made Adam the head over the earth. He gave Adam "dominion" or power and control over the earth. Since Adam was our first leader, everything he did affected everything on earth. We know that God told Adam if he disobeyed he would surely die. So, since Adam had to die because of sin, everything on the earth would also have to die. And that includes all the animals. It wouldn't make sense to have sinful humans who would die when everything else around them remained perfect.

When our dog died, I was sad! But it reminded me how terrible sin is, and because of sin, everything and everyone must die. At the same time, I was joyfully reminded that because of Jesus Christ and His death on the Cross, the people who believe in Him would live forever with Him in heaven even though their bodies may die here on earth.

Romans 8:20-22

Question: If I am God's child, then why doesn't He keep me from being sick or hurt here on earth?

Jonathan S.

Age 10 — Kentucky, USA

22

Answer:

And God will wipe away every tear from their eyes; there shall be no more death, nor sorrow, nor crying. There shall be no more pain, for the former things have passed away (Revelation 21:4).

We often ask questions like: "Why am I sick?" "Why do people have to die?" "Why did my pet die?" Well, Jonathan, this is not the way God created the world to be. You see, after God created everything in the universe, He said it was all very good. If the world had stayed this way, nothing bad would ever have happened. But God created Adam with the ability to choose right and wrong. And even though Adam enjoyed everything in the Garden, and was even the head over all the earth, he still chose to do something terribly wrong. He chose to disobey God. Well, God made it clear that if Adam disobeyed Him by eating the fruit from the tree, then he would die. From that very first sin, all living things would have to die.

Sickness is part of dying. And even when you get sick and then get well again, it is still a reminder that the world is no longer "very good," the way God made it, because we all sin against Him. But there is great news! If you are God's child and believe in Jesus Christ, the Bible says there will one day be a place that is "very good" again; a place without the sickness and death that comes because of sin.

Genesis 1:31; 2:17; 3:6; Romans 8:22

23

Question:  If God can control anything, why did He let the tsunami hit and so many people get hurt? Did He create the tsunami?

Sam W.

Age 7 —Texas, USA

24

Answer:

And they feared exceedingly, and said to one another, "Who can this be, that even the wind and the sea obey Him" (Mark 4:41).

God does control everything that happens on earth and in the universe. He is the Creator of all. He can cause a tsunami and He can will that no tsunami come. But from the Book of Genesis we know that God created all things perfectly. Tsunamis, death, divorce, earthquakes, floods, fighting . . . all the bad things in the world . . . are because of sin. It's not God's fault these things happen — it is because of sin. Sin came into the world through Adam's choice to disobey God — we all sin because of Adam. When we sin, it is like telling God we don't want Him in our lives and that we prefer to do it our way. Terrible things in our lives show us what living without God — without His grace, mercy, and protection — may be like. But those terrible things also show us just how much we need Him!

Please remember, Sam, we are all sinners and sin is the most terrible thing in our lives. Because of our sin against God, bad things happen. It is so amazing that even though we don't deserve it, God sent Jesus who was punished in our place so that we could be forgiven. Those who believe in Jesus will one day live in a place where the bad things will finally be over for good!

Isaiah 45:7

25

Question: Why did Cain Kill Abel?

Calista M.

Age 8 — New Hampshire, U

26

Answer:

...not as Cain who was of the wicked one and murdered his brother. And why did he murder him? Because his works were evil and his brother's righteous (1 John 3:12).

We know that Cain killed Abel. If we look at the Bible account of Cain and Abel we see that they both offered sacrifices. But even though they both offered something to God, their hearts were different. You see, Cain's heart was wicked and evil. God warned Cain that sin would be "at his door" or that sin had a desire for him. This is a reminder to us that sin in our lives is always trying to persuade us to do bad things that dishonor God. This is what happened to Cain. Cain's sacrifice would not have pleased God because of that — no matter what it had been. Now, Abel's heart was faithful and true to God and his sacrifice was excellent in God's eyes. When Cain realized that God was not pleased with his sacrifice but accepted Abel's, his heart became more wicked. He was angry and jealous of his brother and killed him out of envy. Calista, when I read the account of Cain and Abel, I see that God knows our hearts very well. We need to pray that our hearts are pure toward God and when we serve Him, we do it because of the sincere love, honor, and respect we have for Him —not like Cain. Then He will be pleased.

Hebrews 11:4; Genesis 4:3-8

27

Question: What happens to the people who died before Jesus came? Are they in heaven or hell?

Adam S.

Age 8 — Hawaii, USA

28

Answer:

But you have come to Mount Zion and to the city of the living God, the heavenly Jerusalem, to an innumerable company of angels, to the general assembly and church of the firstborn who are registered in heaven, to God the Judge of all, to the spirits of just men made perfect (Hebrews 12:22–23).

Well Adam, Jesus is and has always been the central point of history. In the Old Testament, we read about the law that was given to the Israelites, and all the sacrifices they were commanded by God to carry out, all the festivals they were to keep, and all the feasts they were to conduct. The reason for all of these is that they pointed to Jesus. You see, since the Fall, when sin entered the world, everyone on earth through faith (either in Jesus who was to come or Jesus who has now come) has opportunity for salvation through faith. This is why the Jews had so many laws, festivals, and sacrifices, which now have all been fulfilled in Christ, the Messiah they were looking towards. It would have been impossible for a Jew to do something without it having reference to the Messiah yet to come. Praise God, the Messiah has now come. We all need to make sure we have put our faith and trust in Him.

So the point, Adam, is that people before Christ were saved by faith, and thus went to heaven when they died, and those who did not have faith were separated from God forever.

Hebrews 11:1-12:23, 13 Luke 16:19-25

29

Question: Did Adam and Eve go to heaven?

Danielle F.

30

Answer:

By faith Abel offered to God a more excellent sacrifice than Cain, through which he obtained witness that he was righteous, God testifying of his gifts; and through it he being dead still speaks (Hebrews 11:4).

Well, Danielle, the Bible doesn't say for sure if Adam and Eve went to heaven or believed God's promise of the coming Savior. I think that the Bible shows that it is a good possibility. Look at our verse above from the great faith chapter of Hebrews. God tells us that Abel offered an excellent sacrifice to God, that he had faith, and that he was made righteous. Abel was Adam and Eve's son and it seems that the only way he could have learned about God was from his parents. After all, they walked with God and talked with God. They were the first two humans ever created. They were the first to sin and that sin started the practice of making sacrifices to God for the forgiveness of sins. (Remember how God killed an animal to make clothes for Adam and Eve because they suddenly knew they were naked?) Abel knew how to offer a sacrifice that was pleasing to God. He offered that with a heart that believed in God through faith, and he probably learned that from his parents, Adam and Eve. If all that is true, then it seems as though Adam and Eve knew the truth as well, and if they did, they will be in heaven.

Genesis 2:18; 3:8; 3:21

31

Question: What is heaven like? Are there really mansions? Will I stay ten forever?

Chelsea G.

Age 10 — Virginia, USA

32

Answer:

In My Father's house are many mansions; if it were not so, I would have told you. I go to prepare a place for you. And if I go and prepare a place for you, I will come again and receive you to Myself; that where I am, there you may be also (John 14:2–3).

My dad used to tell me that heaven is where God is and sin is not. In heaven we will see God's glory and worship Him with the angels and heavenly creatures. The Bible refers to mansions in our Father's house. Will there really be mansions? It could be. But whatever Jesus is referring to here, we know that it will be something amazing that our minds can't even imagine. But the most important thing is that Jesus will be there. We know it will be an awesome, beautiful place and really BIG! Unlike anything we have ever seen before! And what about your age? What kind of body will you have? That is not made clear. Let me tell you what the Bible DOES say. The apostle Paul describes the body as a tent. Something that will be destroyed when we die (when our souls go to be with the Lord.) And the Bible tells us that one day we will have new physical bodies that will be different from the bodies we have now. What will the changes be? We don't know for sure. I truly believe it will be something like Jesus' resurrection body!

Matthew 6:9; 2 Peter 3:13; Revelation 21:16-27; 1 Corinthians 15:51-52

HOLY BIBLE

33

Question: How will I know what to do when I get to heaven?

Leah E.

Age 6 — Ohio, USA

34

Answer:

But as it is written: "Eye has not seen, nor ear heard, Nor have entered into the heart of man The things which God has prepared for those who love Him" (1 Corinthians 2:9).

We can't even begin to imagine what heaven will be like and to actually be in the presence of our wonderful God! The Bible tells us that there will be no more crying, no more death, or sorrow, or pain. Everything will be made new, and right, and perfect! Leah, it is a wonderful place God promises for us. But, it is only for those who know, trust, and believe in Jesus Christ our Savior. When you trust in Jesus, believe He died on the Cross for you, and tell Him you are truly sorry for your sins, He will forgive you. That is the only way any of us will ever get to heaven. And here is the important thing Leah — we should not want to get to heaven because we think it is a cool place for us! No, we want to be in heaven because we love God and want to worship Him. Do you know what the people are doing who are already in heaven? The Bible tells us they are glorifying and worshiping God. When we get to heaven we will have perfect love for God and He will be our primary and eternal desire. We will worship Him in full happiness and will never want to stop. That is the day that we should all look for.

Revelation 21:4-5; Psalm 16:11

35

Question: What does being "born again" mean?

Kyle R.

Age 6 — Illinois, US

36

Answer:

Jesus answered and said to him, "Most assuredly, I say to you, unless one is born again, he cannot see the kingdom of God" (John 3:3).

A long time ago, a Jewish ruler (Nicodemus) came to Jesus and asked the very same question. He wondered how in the world a person could be born again when they were already old. Jesus' answer was very clear. Being born again means becoming part of God's family — the word "again" literally means "from above" — becoming a child of God. This is different than being born like a baby is born; this birth is a spiritual birth. It is something that happens in our heart. It is actually becoming a new creation. Let me explain. When I was born again into God's family, my life changed and my heart changed. I knew I was God's child now. The things I wanted to do were different. I wanted to learn about God. I learned to trust Jesus and understood that without Him I could never get to heaven. I wanted to go to church and learn more about what the Bible says. I began to love God more and more (as I got to know Him better). I learned that God hated my sins, but that if I was sorry for them and if I believed that Jesus died on the Cross so I could be forgiven, then God would forgive me. Being born again has given me assurance that I will one day be in heaven with God, my Lord and Savior! It can do the same for you.

John 1:12; 2 Corinthians 5:17; Romans 10:13

Question: When Jesus comes back, why will all of nature (mountains, trees, rocks, etc.) bow down to Him and how will they do that?

Lane T.

Age 10 — Kansas, USA

38

Answer:

For you shall go out with joy,
And be led out with peace;
The mountains and the hills
Shall break forth into singing before you,
And all the trees of the field shall clap their hands (Isaiah 55:12).

Lane, the Bible actually contains 66 different books. It contains different styles of writing. For instance, we know the Book of Genesis is history and tells us exactly what God did. But there are other books, like the Psalms, that are considered poetry. Now poetry is different from history. Poetry can use different words to describe things. When you hear someone say, "It's raining cats and dogs," do you really think that cats and dogs are coming out of the sky? No, it is just the way we talk to describe something we might have a hard time describing otherwise. So when God tells us that the mountains and the hills will cry out and the trees will clap their hands, God is describing joy and delight and praise that is really too great to even imagine. He is saying that people will be filled with joy and will be celebrating! As you continue to study the Bible, you will see that in spite of different styles of writing and the use of some figures of speech, God always conveys His message perfectly.

Proverbs 30:5; Psalm 19:8

39

Question: Why did Jesus preach in the Middle East and not America?

Joy B.

Age 11 — Michigan, US

40

Answer:

Go therefore and make disciples of all the nations, baptizing them in the name of the Father and of the Son and of the Holy Spirit (Matthew 28:19).

When Jesus came to earth, He knew exactly what He had to do. He had a ministry and a plan. Jesus wasn't preaching very long before He called his 12 disciples to join Him. Jesus' message to the people was that He was God and that He was the promised Savior, the one who would save the people from their sins. Jesus preached to the people but also taught His 12 disciples in a special way. After three short years, Jesus was crucified. But before He died, He told His disciples He would send them a Helper (the Holy Spirit) — and He said to go into all the world and preach the gospel. His plan is for people to take the gospel throughout the world. The Helper would give wisdom and courage to continue teaching in Jesus' name. They did receive that wisdom and courage and continued to share the good news about Jesus. They taught more and more people … and those people taught more people . . . and Christianity spread to many nations. So the answer to your question really is that although Jesus only preached in the Middle East, His word is still spreading today as He commanded to happen. The Apostles — the word means "messengers" — took the gospel to the rest of the world because Jesus commanded to take it to Jerusalem, Judea, Samaria, and to the ends of the earth. So the message of salvation came from Jesus, and He commanded it should be spread to the whole planet.

Mark 16:15; Acts 1:8

Question: Did God cry when Jesus died?

Cheyenne

Age 9 — Belgium

42

Answer:

Jesus wept (John 11:35).

The Bible tells us that Jesus wept. He wept at the grave of His friend, Lazarus, and He wept as He drew near the city of Jerusalem for the last time. We know that Jesus is God — that He became a man, was crucified, rose from the dead, and went back to heaven. So when Jesus cried, this was God crying — but it was God in His human form crying. Thus, Cheyenne, we know God has emotions. Now, when Jesus died it was different. Jesus cried to God the Father, "Why have you forsaken me?" At that moment God the Father turned His back on the Son because of our sin. This was always part of God's plan to offer a perfect sacrifice to save those who would believe in Jesus. So was God crying when Jesus died? Well we don't know — but I'm sure He was more sad than we could ever be. Even though it was terrible, God knew that Jesus' obedience to Him on the cross would bring Him glory. God knew that it would complete His plan for eternal life in heaven to anyone who would believe in Jesus and trust Him for forgiveness and salvation.

John 10:30; 11:32–34; 17:3, 5; Luke 19:41; Isaiah 53:10

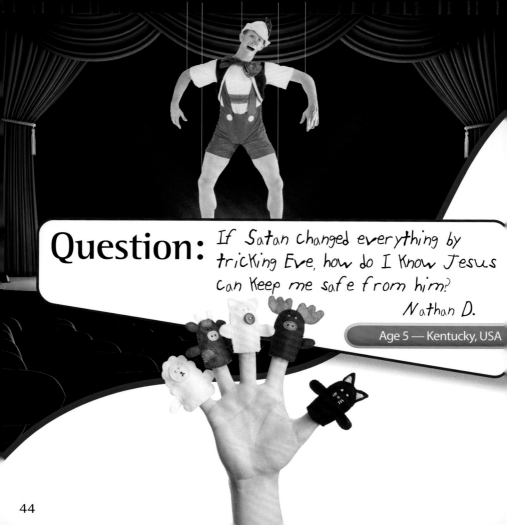

Question: If Satan changed everything by tricking Eve, how do I know Jesus can keep me safe from him?

Nathan D.

Age 5 — Kentucky, USA

44

Answer:

You are of God, little children, and have overcome them, because He who is in you is greater than he who is in the world (1 John 4:4).

Well it wasn't Satan who changed everything — really, it was our sin in Adam that changed everything. When God created Adam and Eve, He didn't make them to be like puppets. He wanted them to enjoy Him, obey Him, and love Him. But we know that Adam and Eve didn't do that. Satan tempted Adam to sin (even though God created him with the ability not to sin). When Jesus was on earth, Satan tempted Him also, but Jesus resisted and overcame Satan, thus sealing his doom. Because of Adam's sin, we all sin (remember Adam was the first human created and God made him the head of the human race) and because we come from him, what he did (sin), we did. We too deserve to be punished for our sin. But don't forget God's wonderful plan of salvation which He had worked out before He created the universe! God wanted to show us how much He loved us by sending His only Son to earth, that whoever believes in Him will share eternal life with Him in heaven! You'll still need to watch out for Satan. He is always trying to get us to disobey God. You can help stop Satan's influence in your life by reading your Bible, believing it, and praying for God's wisdom. Whenever you do sin, tell God you are sorry — as a Christian, your sin has already been forgiven, but we need to learn to be like Jesus every day. When we let God know how sorry we are for our sin, that even helps us recognize the sin problem in our own life !

Romans 3:23; 6:23; John 3:16;
Ephesians 1:13; 1 Peter 5:8

45

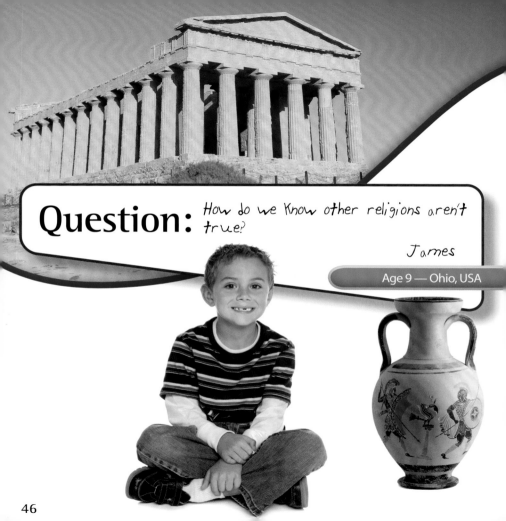

Question:

How do we know other religions aren't true?

James

Age 9 — Ohio, USA

Answer:

Nor is there salvation in any other, for there is no other name under heaven given among men by which we must be saved (Acts 4:12).

No religion other than Christianity has a book like the Bible that tells us about the origin of everything, and who we are, where we came from, what our problem is (sin), and what the solution to our sin problem is. No other religion has a Savior who is alive (He rose from the dead). All other religions require people to do something to work out their future — only Christianity has the solution that we can't save ourselves, only God can do it. So how can we know if other religions aren't true? Well, if they don't agree with the Bible they are not true! There are two main tests I want you to use though. First of all, any religion that claims to be true MUST believe that Jesus is God! Remember, Jesus Himself told us that He and the Father are one. Many religions talk about God a lot . . . but if they don't believe in Jesus and that He is God, and they don't believe that Jesus' death on the cross and His Resurrection results in our sin being forgiven if we will receive it, then it is not the truth! The other test is to find out if they believe that salvation is given to those who trust in Jesus . There is nothing you can do to save yourself. We could never do enough good works to get us to heaven, but Jesus did it when He died for us! Jesus Christ is the way, the truth, and the life.

John 10:30; 14:6; Ephesians 2:8-9

47

Answers Are Always Important!

The Bible is truly filled some amazing answers for some of our toughest faith questions. The Answers Book for Kids series answers questions from children around the world in this multi-volume series. Each volume will answer over 20 questions in a friendly and readable style appropriate for children 6–12 years old; and each covers a unique topic, including Creation and the Fall; Dinosaurs and the Flood of Noah; God and the Bible; Sin, Salvation, and the Christian Life; and more!

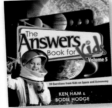

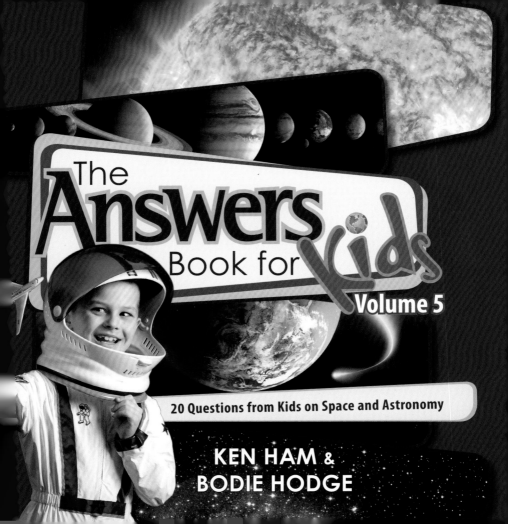

The Answers Book for Kids

Book for Kids

Volume 5

20 Questions from Kids on Space and Astronomy

KEN HAM & BODIE HODGE

Tenth Printing: August 2022

Master Books
P.O. Box 726
Green Forest, AR 72638

Master Books® is a division of the New Leaf Publishing Group, Inc.

Printed in China

Book design by Terry White

ISBN 13: 978-0-89051-782-6
ISBN 13: 978-1-61458-348-6 (digital)
Library of Congress Control Number: 2008904921

All Scripture references are New King James Version unless otherwise noted.

Please visit our website for other great titles: www.masterbooks.com

Special thanks to the kids who contributed from around the world, as well as kids from Cornerstone Classical Christian Academy for their submissions!

When you see this icon, there will be related Scripture references noted for parents to use in answering their children's, and even their own, questions.

Dear Kids,

We hope this book will help answer some of your questions about space and astronomy. We pray that you understand that the Bible is true and that it explains the universe that we live in.

We see many sad things happening in our world. And we all do bad things, too. This is because of sin. Because Adam, our mutual grandfather (about 6,000 years ago), sinned against God and ruined the perfect world God originally created, we suffer and die due to sin, too.

But God provided a means to save us from sin and death. He sent His Son Jesus into the world to become a man and die on our behalf. Christ died on the Cross, but He also rose again (came back to life). If we repent (feel sorry and turn from our sin) and believe in Jesus Christ as our Lord and Savior and in His Resurrection, we too will be saved and get to spend all eternity with God in heaven with all of His goodness. Please read these Scriptures in the order given:

Genesis 1:1, 1:31, 3:17–19; Romans 5:12, 3:23, 6:23, 10:9, 5:1

God bless you.

Ken and Bodie

Question: What day were the planets created?

Kyle

Age 6

4

Answer:

God set them in the firmament of the heavens to give light on the earth (Genesis 1:17).

According to God's Word, bodies out in space, like the sun, moon, and stars, were created on day 4 of the creation week. This is found in Genesis 1:14–19.

God called the sun, the greater light — and it dominates the day. God called the moon, the lesser light — and it dominates the night. Genesis 1:16 says, "He [God] made the stars also." The word that we translate "stars" also includes planets, comets, asteroids, and so on.

Many people incorrectly guess that the solar system and the planets formed from a spinning and collapsing nebula (a cloud of gas and dust) with the sun at the center and the planets, asteroids, and so on at various distances. This has never been observed or repeated; it is just a story to try to explain the universe without God.

God, who knows all things and who was there at the beginning, revealed in His Word that He was responsible for creating the sun, moon, and stars (including the planets). Be careful about the stories that man tells, especially when they disagree with God's Word. "It is better to trust in the LORD than to put confidence in man" (Psalm 118:8).

Romans 11:36

5

Question: What is the purpose of stars?

Paige

Age 9

6

Answer:

The stars actually have several purposes besides the obvious signs and seasons (Genesis 1:14). Here are a few others:

To give light: There are a number of purposes for the stars. One purpose was to give light on the earth (Genesis 1:17). They don't give much light to the earth, like the sun or even the moon does (by reflecting the sun's light to earth), but they do give *enough*. On a dark and clear night, when the moon is not out (called a "new moon"), ask your parents to go outside with you so you can see how much light the stars give on the earth.

For comparison: Another purpose for the stars is comparison. If you look up at the night sky, there are many stars. If you used a telescope, you'd almost see more stars than you could imagine! In Genesis 15:5, God told Abraham to look to the sky and number the stars, if he was able to. Then God said to Abraham that his offspring would be just as numerous as the stars! Wow!

To declare the glory of God: According to the Psalms, the heavens and God's handiwork in them declare the glory of God. At the Creation Museum, we have several planetarium shows, and one takes a look at the size of the universe. It is immense with stars and galaxies (massive clusters of stars). When our guests leave that show after viewing the heavens — the stars, nebulae, and everything else — they usually give the glory to God!

Genesis 1:17; Psalm 136:9; Genesis 15:5;
Deuteronomy 10:22; Psalm 19:1

HOLY BIBLE

Question: Where are the "waters" that are "above" the expanse? Is there water at the edge of the universe?

Sean

Age 11

8

Answer:

Thus God made the firmament, and divided the waters which were under the firmament from the waters which were above the firmament; and it was so (Genesis 1:7).

God created water on day 1 of the creation week. On the second day of creation, God separated the waters by placing an expanse or firmament between these waters. God basically took the water and made some go up and some go down, so that the waters were above and below. Then the waters below were gathered into one place and God called them "seas" on day 3. God called this expanse *between* the waters "heaven," though sometimes this is translated as "sky."

It is basically what is *above* the earth. This would include our atmosphere (inner space) and outer space. It's what you see when you stand outside and look up. There is no doubt that the first clouds (which are droplets of water, not vapor) were made during this expanse. The expanse extends far into space, though we don't know how far it really was. God made the sun, moon, and stars *in* the expanse on day 4 (Genesis 1:17). The universe would have to be really big in order to hold all the stars that are out there.

Genesis 1:6–8, 1:17

sday Friday Tuesday
ursday Sunday
ursday TUESDAY
nday Tues
dnesday
Saturs

Question: Where does a week come from?

Caleb

Age 6

10

Answer:

For in six days the LORD made the heavens and the earth, the sea, and all that is in them, and rested the seventh day. Therefore the LORD blessed the Sabbath day and hallowed it (Exodus 20:11).

This question is very important! Let's look at some *other* time references (days, months, and years) first. A day is one rotation of the earth on its axis. A month ultimately comes from one revolution of the moon around the earth. A year comes from one revolution of the earth around the sun. A week (7 days) has nothing to do with *any* astronomical time reference. So where does a week come from? A week comes from the Bible, because God created in 6 days and He rested on the seventh day.

God, being God, didn't need to rest. He did that for our benefit. In Exodus 20:11, God explains that He created in 6 days and rested for one day as a basis for our workweek. This is why everyone works according to this pattern. Moses and the Israelites worked for 6 days and then rested on the seventh day (called the "Sabbath"). Exodus 31:17 is another confirmation that God created in six normal days and not over the millions and billions of years taught in the secular media and education system. God's Word can be trusted over any of these false myths that the earth is millions of years old.

Exodus 20:11, 31:17; 1 Timothy 4:7

11

Question: What are black holes?

Lane

Age 10

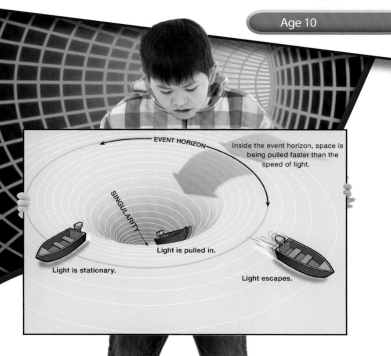

EVENT HORIZON

Inside the event horizon, space is being pulled faster than the speed of light.

SINGULARITY

Light is pulled in.

Light is stationary.

Light escapes.

Answer:

For by Him all things were created that are in heaven and that are on earth, visible and invisible, whether thrones or dominions or principalities or powers. All things were created through Him and for Him (Colossians 1:16).

Black holes are real objects that God made in space. Because they have so much mass, their gravity is so strong that light can't even escape from them. If light cannot escape a black hole, then it can never get to your eyes, so it appears black. When you close your eyes in a dark room, you can't see anything, and it appears black because light doesn't make it to your eye.

A black hole's gravity is so strong that it pulls light back into it. Imagine throwing a ball up into the sky — it would fall back down again, right?

In a black hole, it is actually doing more than just pulling *light* in. It is actually pulling *space itself* in faster than the speed of light. So light that is trying to travel away from a black hole moving at the speed of light gets sucked into it.

In a black hole, there is a certain distance away from it where the trend reverses and light is faster and can escape. That distance is called the "event horizon." But a black hole actually distorts the space around itself. Researchers recently found what they think is the largest black hole ever discovered. It's at the core of the galaxy called "NGC 1277."

*Colossians 1:6; Nehemiah 9:6;
Revelation 21:1*

13

Question: Is it possible that there are living things in space?

Becca

Age 9

14

Answer:

For thus says the LORD, Who created the heavens, Who is God, Who formed the earth and made it, Who has established it, Who did not create it in vain, Who formed it to be inhabited: "I am the LORD, and there is no other (Isaiah 45:18).

Yes — there are people living on the space station right now. But they came from earth! The Bible seems to rule out any native intelligent life in outer space since they would be under the Curse with no possibility of salvation (Romans 8). Only the descendants of Adam can be saved (1 Corinthians 15:22–45). Earth was the center of life that God made in six days. God made the earth livable or habitable (Isaiah 45:18), and God never said other places in space were habitable. When Christ returns, it will be on the earth and nowhere else.

Of course, there are beings like angels, cherubim, and other heavenly host that are viewed as spiritual life in heaven. God *is* spirit (John 4:24), so it makes sense that He can make life in both physical and spiritual forms. We, as people, have a body *and* a spirit.

Spaceships, satellites, and probes have taken all sorts of bacteria to space when they didn't mean to. Surely some probes to places like Mars were not absent of bacteria. Many little microbes could also be whisked into space from our upper atmosphere. But keep in mind that these all originated on earth.

John 4:24; Isaiah 45:18

15

Question: Is Jupiter stormy?

Grant

Age 7

16

Answer:

Fire and hail, snow and clouds; stormy wind, fulfilling His word
(Psalm 148:8).

Jupiter is the largest planet in our solar system. Unlike Mercury, Venus, Earth, and Mars, Jupiter is a giant gas planet, but deep inside it is likely made of rock and metallic gasses that have been compressed and solidified. The stripes that appear on the planet are actually generated by strong winds. Because of its gas composition and strong winds, it is prone to massive storms.

The biggest storm on Jupiter is called the Great Red Spot, and it appears as a large red spot on the planet. It's a storm that has been raging for a long time — it has been observed continuously since the 1800s. Imagine being stuck inside your house for an almost 200-year-long storm! We are not sure if God created Jupiter with the Great Red Spot storm, or if the storm started after God initially created everything. There would not be a problem in a perfect world before Adam and Eve sinned to have a storm like this on a planet that doesn't have life.

Jupiter is actually a rather hot planet. It gives off more heat energy than it receives. This is important because some people incorrectly think that Jupiter is billions of years old. If it were, it should have cooled off by now. But if it were created about 6,000 years ago, this explains why it still has heat to give off.

Job 26:12; Psalm 107:25

Question: What are comets and what are they made of?

Neva

Age 8

18

Answer:

Thus God made the firmament, and divided the waters which were under the firmament from the waters which were above the firmament; and it was so (Genesis 1:7).

Comets are icy objects in space that release dust or gas when they approach the sun. They are typically made of ice, dust, and frozen gases, and some even have a rocky core. Comets are very small compared to a planet and usually have highly elliptical (egg-shaped) orbits.

Some comets are called "sun-grazers." They completely disintegrate when they get close to the sun; they may even crash right into it! When a comet nears the sun, it heats up and the gases and ice break off of the comet, making it smaller and leaving a beautiful trail of debris. This is where meteor showers come from. When the earth passes through the previous path of a comet, these pieces burn up as they fall into our atmosphere. This means that comets can't last billions of years and this is a good confirmation that the solar system (including comets) is not that old.

The age of creation is based on the Bible's genealogies. When we calculate the numbers in these genealogies, we get an age around 6,000 years (e.g., 4,000 years from creation to Christ). Comets make sense in a young solar system.

Genesis 5:3–5

Question: How far away is the next galaxy?

Tallia

Age 9

20

Answer:

For as the heavens are higher than the earth, so are My ways higher than your ways, and My thoughts than your thoughts (Isaiah 55:9).

A galaxy is a system that usually consists of billions of stars held together by gravity. We see them far away and near our own galaxy. Our galaxy is called the Milky Way. The nearest galaxy depends on how we define a galaxy. There are masses of stars much smaller than the Milky Way that are considered a galaxy. There are many of these, and the close ones are also considered satellites of our own Milky Way galaxy. Think of all the moons, which are satellites that surround Jupiter. The smaller masses of stars are satellites to the Milky Way just like those moons are satellites of Jupiter.

If we count these satellites of the Milky Way as galaxies, then the next closest galaxy is Canis Major Dwarf, which is about 25,000 light years away. Of course, astronomers still debate about the specifics and classification of these minor galaxies, including this one. There are about 19 satellite galaxies in the next major galaxy, called Andromeda Galaxy (M31). But it would be the closest galaxy that is about the size of the Milky Way (200,000 light years across). In fact, it is a little larger than the Milky Way, and it shares the same spiral shape. Spiral galaxies are good examples of why the universe is not billions of years old. If they were, the spiral arms should have all been wound up already!

Ecclesiastes 3:11; Job 22:12; Psalm 147:4

HOLY BIBLE

Question:

How many planets are there? What is the smallest planet? Could planets hit each other?

Jackson, Gershom, & Annie

Ages 9, 8, & 10

22

Answer:

Can you bind the cluster of the Pleiades, or loose the belt of Orion? (Job 38:31).

The definition of a planet was recently changed. Because of this change, the previous count of nine planets was changed to eight. Pluto is no longer considered a planet. According to the new definition, a planet must be massive enough to be nearly round, in orbit around the sun (usually in the same basic plane), and have control of its surroundings (e.g., moons, rings, and so on revolve around it.) By this definition, there are only eight planets (Mercury, Venus, Earth, Mars, Jupiter, Saturn, Uranus, and Neptune). Although Pluto used to be considered the smallest planet, the smallest one is now Mercury. Mercury is also the closest planet to the sun.

Planets have a fixed orbit at a certain distance around the sun, so none of them will ever collide. They are very far away from each other. There are things that collide with planets and moons, but these are smaller chunks of rock, like meteoroids. The orbits of some other items like comets *could* hit planets. They have an orbit that comes close to the sun and then travels far away from it. These could hit a planet, but it would still be a very rare event since the solar system is big and even planets are very small in this big system, but it does happen from time to time. For example, in 1994, Jupiter was hit by Comet Shoemaker-Levy 9.

Psalm 108:5; Psalm 57:11

23

Question: Did Christians believe the earth was flat?

Kylie

Age 6

24

Answer:

It is He who sits above the circle of the earth, and its inhabitants are like grasshoppers, who stretches out the heavens like a curtain, and spreads them out like a tent to dwell in (Isaiah 40:22).

Most ancients believed in a round earth including Christians. Eratosthenes was an ancient geographer who even calculated the circumference of the earth about 200 B.C.! Very few Christians ever believed that the earth was flat. One Christian who did believe this was Lactantius (ca. A.D. 240–300). Sadly, he mixed the false flat-earth concept with his Christianity.

An overwhelming number of Christians opposed a flat earth, and for good reason. The Bible teaches against it in Isaiah 40:22 and Job 26:10. These verses point out that the earth is circular or round. Job even goes so far as to say that the earth hangs on nothing (Job 26:7)! This was confirmed when we sent satellites and people into space, and they could see and take pictures of the earth simply "hanging on nothing."

From the big picture though, Christians should always be careful about taking ideas that come from outside Scripture and mixing them with their Christianity. Instead, we should trust what God's Word says, since He knows best!

Isaiah 40:22; Job 26:7, 10

25

Question: Do meteors burn up and are they dangerous?

Simeon & Zachary

Ages 10 & 7

26

Answer:

Do not be overly wicked, nor be foolish: why should you die before your time? (Ecclesiastes 7:17).

Meteors are made from meteoroids and sometimes asteroids, which are bigger. Meteoroids are rocky and/or icy fragments (depending on comet remnants) that are smaller than asteroids and are found in many parts of space. Meteoroids, when they fall into earth's atmosphere, become "meteors." If some parts of a meteor don't burn up (due to the heated compression of the air in front of the meteor), those pieces are called "meteorites." Can they be dangerous? Yes, they can, but most are not. Most meteors typically burn up, with nothing left of them to fall out of the sky. It's actually rather enjoyable to watch as the meteors burn up — we often call the flashes of light across the night sky "falling stars" or "shooting stars," even though they are not really stars. But if the pieces are large and do not burn up all the way, then they can hit the ground really fast, sending a big shockwave! This can do serious damage.

A meteor that was about 50 feet in diameter (15 meters) hit the city of Chelyabinsk, Russia, on February 15, 2013. Much of the meteor burned up, but the rest of it shattered above the city and caused a lot of damage with the debris and shockwave. This rare event injured about 1,500 people.

Ecclesiastes 3:1; Romans 8:22

27

Question: How hot are the sun and other stars?

Eve

Age 8

Answer:

For no sooner has the sun risen with a burning heat than it withers the grass; its flower falls, and its beautiful appearance perishes. So the rich man also will fade away in his pursuits (James 1:11).

The sun is not too hot or too cold when compared to other stars. Typically, there is a range of temperatures for stars. Blue ones are much hotter, and red ones are much cooler. The surface temperature of the sun is about 10,000° Fahrenheit (or 5505° Celsius and 5778° Kelvin [K]).

The coolest stars (under 3500°K) are red. Next on the scale are red-to-orange stars, with a temperature of 3500–5000°K. Then there are yellow-to-white stars, which range from 5000–6000°K. This is where our sun would be, since it has an average surface temperature of 5778°K. Next are stars in the white-to-blue range, with temperatures of 6000°K — 7500°K.

Blue stars are the hottest (typically over 7500°K) and have three classes: A, B, and O. "A" contains temperatures above 7500°K, "B" contains temperatures over 11,000°K, and O contains temperatures over 25,000°K. The hotter the stars are, the more light they give off (known as luminosity).

Blue stars are a problem for those who believe in millions of years. Blue stars give off so much energy and burn their fuel so fast that they should not be able to last for long periods of time. But a recent creation of about 6,000 years helps to make sense of blue stars.

1 Corinthians 15:41

29

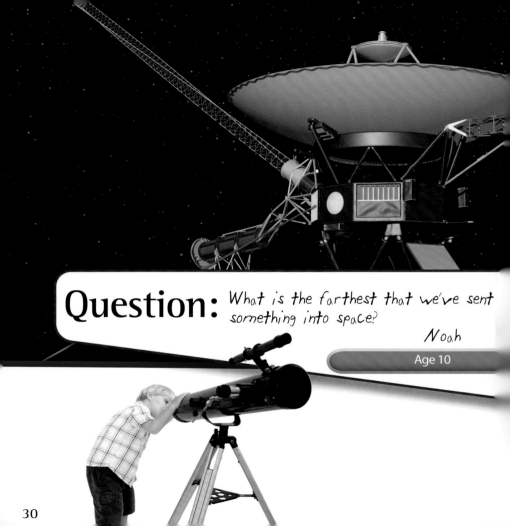

Question: What is the farthest that we've sent something into space?

Noah

Age 10

Answer:

And then He will send His angels, and gather together His elect from the four winds, from the farthest part of earth to the farthest part of heaven (Mark 13:27).

At this stage, we have sent something that has finally reached the outer edges of our solar system and is about to enter interstellar space. It is called the *Voyager 1* spacecraft. Launched in September of 1977 with the goal of studying the outer solar system, it routinely sends back data and pictures. This is easily the farthest that man has ever sent anything into space — and it is still working today! Interestingly, *Voyager 1* was supposed to study Jupiter, Saturn, and their associated moons, rings, and so on. When that was accomplished in November of 1980, the probe simply continued to travel to space. *Voyager 1* is not the only space probe that has been sent to the outer reaches of the solar system. In total, there have been four: *Voyager 1*, *Voyager 2*, *Pioneer 10*, and *Pioneer 11*. *Voyager 2* went to Jupiter, Saturn, Uranus, and Neptune. *Voyager 2* was the only spacecraft to visit Uranus and Neptune, and it is still going, though not as fast as *Voyager 1*.

Man has always been fascinated with finding out what is beyond, and yet so often we miss that the Creator Himself became a man (Jesus Christ) and came to seek us out. Let's not forget that.

Isaiah 55:9; Ephesians 4:10; Luke 19:10

31

Question: What are the rings of planets made from?

Walton

Age 10

32

Answer:

For You are my rock and my fortress; therefore, for Your name's sake, lead me and guide me (Psalms 31:3).

Many planets have moons that orbit them. God has blessed the earth with one moon. But some planets even have beautiful rings that encircle them!

When we talk about planets with rings around them, Saturn is obviously the one many people think of. It is called the "Jewel of the Solar System." The rings are large and bright, so they are easy to see with a telescope. Galileo was the first to discover that Saturn had rings in 1610, though he was confused as to what they were. He was using very limited telescopes he had made.

But our solar system actually has four planets that have rings. Jupiter has rings (discovered in 1979), but they are very faint. Uranus has rings (discovered in 1977), as does Neptune (discovered in 1968 and 1984, but confirmed in 1989). Each ring orbits at a different speed, and each ring and gap or division between the rings are given names, too.

The rings are made up of dust, rock, and ice. Some of the particles are smaller than grains of sand but can be as large as a building.

Colossians 1:15–17

33

Question: What about the big bang?

Kylie

Age 6

Answer:

You alone are the LORD; You have made heaven, the heaven of heavens, with all their host, the earth and everything on it .... The host of heaven worships You (Nehemiah 9:6).

The supposed big bang is one of the popular atheistic models about the origin of the universe. It basically teaches that the universe created itself. There was nothing, then something popped into existence from nothing, rapidly "exploded," and is still expanding today. Actually, biblical creationists expect the heavens to be stretching out as well, but by the power of God, not by a big bang. There are big problems with the big-bang model. First, it conflicts with God's Word. The big-bang model has stars coming into existence before the earth, but God says the earth came before the stars. Also, according to the Bible, the age of the universe is about 6,000 years. This clearly disagrees with the billions of years required for the big bang.

The big bang has several scientific problems, too. Some well-meaning Christians have suggested that maybe God used the big bang, but if that were the case, then God really didn't do anything — and it contradicts His Word. The God of the Bible was intimately involved in creation from the very first verse of the Bible. The issue is whether we will trust a perfect God's Word when He speaks or imperfect human opinions about the past.

Isaiah 42:5, 44:24; Zechariah 12:1;
Colossians 2:8

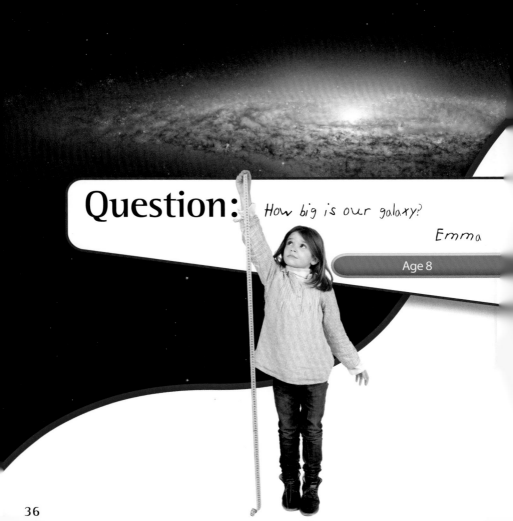

Question: How big is our galaxy?

Emma

Age 8

Answer:

But will God indeed dwell on the earth? Behold, heaven and the heaven of heavens cannot contain You. How much less this temple which I have built! (1 Kings 8:27).

Our galaxy is very big. A galaxy is not the universe, which is much bigger and contains all the galaxies. Our galaxy is called the Milky Way. It is about 120,000 light years across (1 light year = almost 5.878625 trillion miles). It is thought that 200 — 400 billion stars are within the Milky Way.

Compared to other galaxies, the Milky Way is actually a middle-sized one. There are some very large galaxies with stars estimated in the trillions.

There are smaller galaxies, too. Some are so small and near our own galaxy so they are considered satellites of the Milky Way. The stars used for constellations (like Orion, Bear, and Pleiades) are found within our own galaxy. Very few things can be seen with the naked eye outside of our galaxy, but there are a few things like the Andromeda Galaxy and Magellanic Clouds.

Job 9:9; Job 38:31;
Amos 5:8

Question: Will the sun ever run out or blow up?

Emma & Becca

Ages 8 & 9

38

Answer:

They shall fear You as long as the sun and moon endure, throughout all generations (Psalms 72:5).

God is an excellent designer! When He created all things, they were perfect (Genesis 1:31; Deuteronomy 32:4). There was no death, bloodshed, suffering . . . and no homework! The world really was perfect. But it wasn't just the world that was perfect — everything was, including the sun. It was perfectly designed by God. It has been consistently producing light and heat for earth since its creation on day 4 ("the greater light to rule the day"). There is no reason to assume that it will not continue to perform these duties until the end.

Keep in mind something that happened in the past that affects the whole of creation (Romans 8:20–22): the Curse. When Adam sinned against God, God cursed the ground and the animals and sentenced man to die (Genesis 3). The Curse affected everything (Romans 8:22). This would also affect the sun. This is why we will eventually need a new heavens and a new earth (Isaiah 66:17–22; 2 Peter 3:13; Revelation 21:1).

But until then, as long as the earth endures, God promised that day and night, cold and heat, seedtime and harvest, and winter and summer shall not cease (Genesis 8:22). So the sun, which is vital for this, will continue to do its created duties until the end.

Genesis 1:31, 8:22; Romans 8:22; 2 Peter 3:13

Question: What would happen if a comet ran into an asteroid?

Noah

Age 9

40

Answer:

For since the creation of the world His invisible attributes are clearly seen, being understood by the things that are made, even His eternal power and Godhead, so that they are without excuse (Romans 1:20).

Comets are made mostly of dust, rock, and ice, while asteroids are primarily made of rock. A snowball hitting a rock might be similar to what it would be like if a comet hit an asteroid at high speed. The frozen water on a comet vaporizes when the comet nears the sun and makes a comet tail that points away from the sun (called a "coma"). This would make it easier for a comet to break apart than an asteroid. So the comet, depending on the size, would likely be the one that broke up more.

Interestingly, NASA had a mission to smash into a comet. The comet, Tempel 1, was a city-sized comet that was discovered in 1867 by Ernst Tempel. It orbits the sun every 5.5 years. NASA decided to collide an object into it called an "impactor" the size of a small desk that weighed 820 pounds (370 kg.)! This impactor was monitored by a spacecraft called *Deep Impact* to get a glimpse of what was below the surface of the comet.

Many researchers on this mission were hoping to learn a little more about "an evolutionary history" instead of the true history in the Book of Genesis. God's creation is incredible to explore!

Genesis 1:14

41

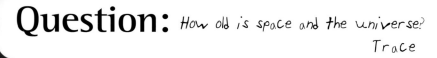

Question: How old is space and the universe?

Trace

Age 6

Answer:

In the beginning God created the heavens and the earth (Genesis 1:1).

The "heavens and the earth" were created by God at the beginning, when He created time (Genesis 1:1) on day 1 of the creation week. There is no word for "universe" in Hebrew, which is the language of the Old Testament. But when "heavens" and "earth" are used together like this, it means the whole of creation, which includes the universe (and space).

God created the universe on day 1 and Adam on day 6. When we add up the genealogies in the Bible from Adam to Abraham in Genesis 5 and 11, it comes to about 2,000 years. Most people agree that Abraham lived about 2,000 B.C., which is approximately 4,000 years ago from today. So we know the universe is around 6,000 years old.

Some try to say the age of the universe is 13–15 billion years! This date comes from people who make assumptions about the past and ignore the Bible's account of creation. You can either trust an all-knowing, perfect God about His creation, or you can trust imperfect people's guesses about the past. God is always right, and if people ever disagree with God's Word, then they are the ones who are wrong. God and His Word are trustworthy and true from the very first verse.

Genesis 1:1; Isaiah 42:5;
Hebrews 11:3

43

Yearly Meteor Shower Dates

Name	Approximate Date Range	Likely Peak
Quadrantids	January 2–3	January 3
Lyrids	April 20–22	April 22
Eta Aquarids	May 4–6	May 6
Delta Aquarids	July 29–30	July 29
Perseids	August 10–13	August 12
Draconids	October 7–10	October 8
Orionids	October 18–23	October 22
Leonids	November 16–18	November 18
Taurids	November 8–10	November 18
Geminids	December 10–12	December 14

Table of Planets and the first 5 *Dwarf Planets*

	Planet or Dwarf Planet	Average distance from the sun (in millions of miles)	Moons	Average Length of year in earth days/years
Mercury	Planet	36	0	88 days
Venus	Planet	67	0	224.7 days
Earth	Planet	93	1	1 year
Mars	Planet	142	2	687 days
Jupiter	Planet	484	67	11.9 years
Saturn	Planet	888	62	27.9 years
Uranus	Planet	1,784	27	84.3 years
Neptune	Planet	2,799	13	164.8 years
Pluto	Dwarf Planet	3,670	5	248 years
Eris	Dwarf Planet	10,180	1	557 years
Haumea	Dwarf Planet	6,432	2	282 years
Makemake	Dwarf Planet	4,214	0	310 years
Ceres	Dwarf Planet	413	0	4.6 years

Definitions

asteroids: Rocky bodies too small to be planets, usually with an irregular shape. There is a large asteroid belt that orbits the sun between Mars and Jupiter. Many asteroids are found throughout our solar system.

meteoroids: Rocky fragments even smaller than asteroids, found in many parts of space. Many are even intermingled in the asteroid belt. When meteoroids fall into earth's atmosphere, they become meteors. If some parts o don't burn up, those pieces are called meteorites.

comets: Objects made mostly of ice, frozen gas, dust, and rock that make lo elliptical orbits around the sun. A comet usually leaves a debris tail a approaches the sun and heats up. The tail of a comet always stretc away from the sun.

planets: Must be massive enough to be nearly round, in orbit around the (usually in the same basic plane), and have control of its surroundi (e.g., moons, rings, and so on revolve around it). By this current definit there are only eight planets (Mercury, Venus, Earth, Mars, Jupiter, Sat Uranus, and Neptune).

dwarf planets: Dwarf planets do not fulfill all the requirements of a planet bu significantly larger than asteroids. Two dwarf planets were at time classed as planets: Ceres and Pluto.

alaxies: Systems of billions of stars held together by gravity. Our solar system is in the Milky Way galaxy, which is a spiral galaxy. Many galaxies that are not spiral have shapes like elliptical, round, toothpick, and ring shapes, among many others.

ebulas: Large cloud-like structures (interstellar) made of dust and gases that give off light in beautiful arrays and shapes. They can be many light-years across.

uasar: Quasar stands for "quasi-stellar radio source." They are among the most distant and brightest (luminous) objects we know of. They emit immense amounts of energy as well. There is still much to learn about quasars.

ht-year: A measure of distance, not time. One light-year is how far light can travel in one year. This is roughly 5,878,625,000,000 miles or 9,460,730,000,000 km.

Answers Are Always Important!

The Bible is truly filled some amazing answers for some of our toughest faith questions. The Answers Book for Kids series answers questions from children around the world in this multi-volume series. Each volume will answer over 20 questions in a friendly and readable style appropriate for children 6–12 years old; and each cover a unique topic, including Creation and the Fall; Dinosaurs and the Flood of Noah; God and the Bible; Sin, Salvation, and the Christian Life; and more!

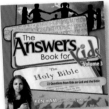

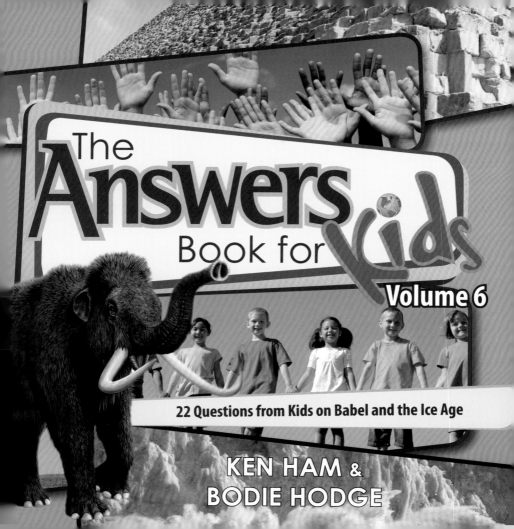

The Answers Book for Kids

Book for Kids

Volume 6

22 Questions from Kids on Babel and the Ice Age

KEN HAM &
BODIE HODGE

Ninth Printing: December 2022

Master Books
P.O. Box 726
Green Forest, AR 72638

Master Books® is a division of the New Leaf Publishing Group, Inc.

Printed in China

Book design by Terry White

ISBN 13: 978-0-89051-783-3
ISBN 13: 978-1-61458-349-3 (digital)
Library of Congress Control Number: 2008904921

All Scripture references are New King James Version unless otherwise noted.

Please visit our website for other great titles: www.masterbooks.com

Special thanks to the kids who contributed from around the world, as well as th
kids from Cornerstone Classical Christian Academy for their submissions!

When you see this icon, there will be related Scripture references
noted for parents to use in answering their children's, and even their
own, questions.

Dear Kids

We hope this book will help answer some of your questions about the Ice Age and the Tower of Babel. We pray that you understand that the Bible is true and that it does explain the world that we live in.

We see a lot of sad things happening in our world, and we all do bad things, too. This is because of sin. When Adam, our mutual grandfather (6,000 years ago), sinned against God and ruined the perfect world God originally created, death and suffering entered the world — so we suffer and die as well because of sin.

But God provided a means to save us from sin and death. He sent His Son Jesus into the world to become a man, live a sinless life, and die on our behalf. He died on a Cross, but He was also resurrected (brought back to life). If we repent (turn from our sin) and believe in Jesus Christ as our Lord and Savior and in His Resurrection, we too will be saved and will spend all eternity with God in heaven with all of His goodness. Please read these Scriptures in this order:

Genesis 1:1, 1:31, 3:17–19; Romans 5:12, 3:23, 6:23, 10:9, 5:1

God bless you.
Ken and Bodie

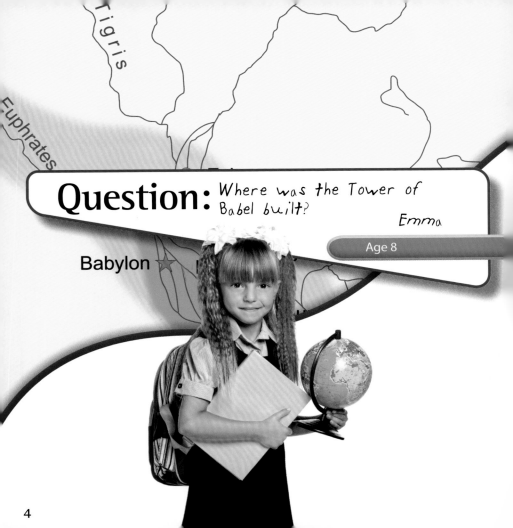

Question: Where was the Tower of Babel built?

Emma

Age 8

Babylon ☆

4

Answer:

And it came to pass, as they journeyed from the east, that they found a plain in the land of Shinar, and they dwelt there (Genesis 11:2).

The tower was built at Babel. This was where Noah's descendants settled after they left Noah's home (where he had become a farmer). They traveled from the east and arrived at a place that they called Shinar (shee-NAR), which means "between two rivers."

These two rivers were the Tigris and Euphrates. These rivers formed as a result of Noah's Flood, and were likely named for two pre-Flood rivers that were mentioned in Genesis 2:14. This re-using of familiar names has happened many times down through the ages. For instance, when the Europeans came to the Americas they named rivers, cities, and regions after places in Europe.

Noah's descendants found a plain between these rivers and dwelt there. That plain is where Babel was located. This small city of Babel and the region of Babylonia (the region was later named after the city of Babel) were in southern Mesopotamia, which is part of modern-day Iraq. Later, the city of Babel (or Babylon) became the same site where a big empire was based — the Babylonian Empire, led by Nebuchadnezzar.

The city of Babel was located along the Euphrates River in the plain of Shinar, south of the modern city of Baghdad in Iraq.

2 Kings 20:14; Daniel 11:1

HOLY BIBLE

Question: How big was the Tower of Babel?

Gershom

Age 8

6

Answer:

And they said, "Come, let us build ourselves a city, and a tower whose top is in the heavens; let us make a name for ourselves, lest we be scattered abroad over the face of the whole earth" (Genesis 11:4).

The Bible doesn't tell us how big the Tower of Babel was. It is described as "a tower whose top is in the heavens" (Genesis 11:4). This means that it was much taller than the buildings of the city that Noah's descendants were constructing. The tower would have been above them, but it would not have needed to be as big as a skyscraper today. Later, other towers were built in the same area that had names similar to "tower whose top is in the heavens", but these towers were not that big. They were just the largest structures compared to what was around them.

Many believe that the Etemenanki (EH-tuh-meh-NAHN-kee) tower was simply another later name for the Tower of Babel. Etemenanki means "temple of the foundation of heaven and earth." The tower was old and run down by the time of Daniel and Nebuchadnezzar (500– 600 B.C.) and Alexander the Great tore it down about 325 B.C.

Judging by the square base where the tower originally was located, an old description on a tablet, and the writing of a historian named Herodotus, the tower was probably about 7–8 stories and 300 feet (91 meters) high. That would definitely be big enough to stand out in a little city!

Genesis 11:3–4; Judges 9:51;
Proverbs 18:10

Question:

How long did it take to build the Tower of Babel?

Eva

Age 8

8

Answer:

Then they said to one another, "Come, let us make bricks and bake them thoroughly." They had brick for stone, and they had asphalt for mortar (Genesis 11:3).

The Bible doesn't tell us how long it took to build the Tower of Babel, but when people are dedicated to doing something and are working toward the same goal, they can do things very quickly.

For example, Richard the Lionheart, who was king of England in the Middle Ages, had his soldiers build a castle for him in Normandy (a part of France that he ruled). It needed to be built quickly so he could use it. This huge and incredible castle was built in about one year! The ruins of this castle (Chateau Gaillard) still stand today, and they are still very impressive.

A tower would be much easier to build than a complicated castle. A Jewish historian named Josephus, who lived about 2,000 years ago, said of the Tower of Babel, "It grew very high, sooner than anyone could expect."

The people who built the Tower of Babel in Genesis 11:3–6 were dedicated to the cause of building the tower. It may have been built very quickly, possibly in just a few months — but we don't know for sure.

Genesis 11:3-6

9

Question: How many people did it take to build the Tower?

Laura

Age 8

10

Answer:

These were the families of the sons of Noah, according to their generations, in their nations; and from these the nations were divided on the earth after the flood (Genesis 10:32).

The Bible in Genesis 10 gives a list of families that came out of Babel with new languages. Since we don't know how many people were in each family, we can't know the exact number of people who came out of Babel. If we add up the families, there were at least 78. There could have been a few more, since the line that goes from Noah to Peleg (ultimately the line of Jesus) doesn't give us all the information. For example, this line contains Noah, Shem, Arphaxad, Selah, Eber, and Peleg. (Some of these sound like strange names, huh?)

But Genesis 11:13 says that Arphaxad had other children. Genesis 11:14 says that Selah had other children. And Genesis 11:17 says that Eber had other children as well. So these families that were not listed specifically in Genesis 10, but mentioned in Genesis 11, may have had a new language and would add to those 78 families. If each of these 78 families had a dad, a mom, and three kids, that would be just under 400 people! One person named Joktan had 13 kids (Genesis 10:26–29). So some families may have had much more than just three children.

Genesis 9:1; Genesis 11:4

Question: What time period was the Tower of Babel built in?

Noah

Age 9

Big Picture of World History

Columbus rediscovers America	A.D. 1496
Normans conquer England	A.D. 1066
Rome loses power to Constantinople	A.D. 324
Jerusalem and the Temple are destroyed	A.D. 70
Christ was born	4 B.C.
Last book of the Old Testament (Malachi)	416 B.C.
Time of the Kings (Saul was first)	1095 B.C.
Time of the Judges (Moses was first)	1491 B.C.
Call of Abraham	1922 B.C.
Tower of Babel	2242 B.C.
Global Flood	2348 B.C.
Curse	4004 B.C.
Creation	4004 B.C.

12

Answer:

Now this is the genealogy of the sons of Noah: Shem, Ham, and Japheth. And sons were born to them after the flood (Genesis 10:1).

The Tower of Babel incident occurred around 4,200 years ago — about 100 years after the Flood but before Abraham was born, This was before ancient Egypt, Greece, and other early civilizations. These places couldn't have begun until after people left Babel to establish these other civilizations.

Noah's grandson Javan founded Greece. When we read "Greece" in the Old Testament, it is actually the name Javan, which we translate as "Greece." Noah's grandson Mizraim founded Egypt. When we read "Egypt" in the Old Testament, it is the name Mizraim that we translate as "Egypt." Famous and ancient civilizations you are familiar with couldn't have existed until after Babel. This means the Tower of Babel was built prior to the appearance of these ancient cultures.

Genesis 10:32; Genesis 12:10;
Galatians 3:28

13

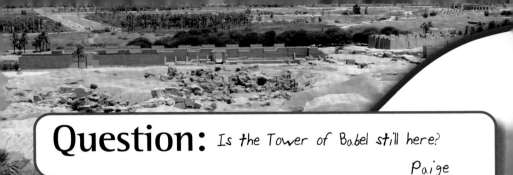

Question: Is the Tower of Babel still here?

Paige

Age 9

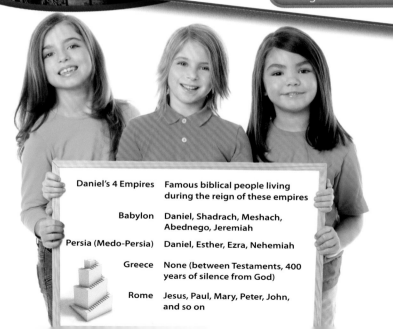

Daniel's 4 Empires	Famous biblical people living during the reign of these empires
Babylon	Daniel, Shadrach, Meshach, Abednego, Jeremiah
Persia (Medo-Persia)	Daniel, Esther, Ezra, Nehemiah
Greece	None (between Testaments, 400 years of silence from God)
Rome	Jesus, Paul, Mary, Peter, John, and so on

14

Answer:

So the LORD scattered them abroad from there over the face of all the earth, and they ceased building the city (Genesis 11:8).

The Tower of Babel is not around anymore. If it were, it would be over 4,200 years old. There are not too many things that can last that long, even if they are made from baked bricks!

The Tower of Babel was said to be an old run-down building over 2,500 years ago. The ruler of the Babylonian Empire, Nebuchadnezzar, wanted to tear it down and rebuild it. But he didn't get an opportunity to. He said:

"Since a remote time, people had abandoned it, without order expressing their words. Since that time earthquakes and lightning had dispersed its sun-dried clay; the bricks of the casing had split, and the earth of the interior had been scattered in heaps."

After the Babylonian Empire, other empires came to power. Daniel, who lived during the same time as Nebuchadnezzar (and lived into the Persian Empire), prophesied about these kingdoms in Daniel 2.

Alexander the Great, who was the founder of the third empire (Greece), did tear down the Tower of Babel. He also wanted to rebuild it. But Alexander died at a very young age, before he could rebuild it, so the tower passed into history.

Job 3:14; Daniel 3:28;
Daniel 4:27

Question: Are there any archaeological remains of the Tower of Babel?

Becca and Brianna

Age 9 & 7

Answer:

With kings and counselors of the earth, who built ruins for themselves (Job 3:14).

There really isn't much left of the Tower of Babel. Alexander the Great removed bricks and the outer coating, but he never rebuilt it. However, most researchers think they know where the foundation is located.

Also, there was an archaeological artifact found called a "stele." A stele (pronounced the same as steal or steel) is actually a rock slab with pictures and inscriptions on it. Archaeologists love finding things like this.

The Tower of Babel stele has an image of Nebuchadnezzar next to the Tower of Babel. It shows its shape as a ziggurat (imagine a step pyramid or a pyramid with several flat layers on it).

About 440 B.C., a historian named Herodotus claimed he saw the tower and described it:

"It has a solid central tower, one furlong square, with a second erected on top of it and then a third, and so on up to eight. All eight towers can be climbed by a spiral way running around the outside, and about halfway up there are seats for those who make the journey to rest on."

This is a great confirmation of the Bible's truthfulness about the Tower of Babel. But remember, the ultimate reason we can know the Tower of Babel existed is because God's Word is true!

2 Kings 19:25

Question: Was there anything inside the Tower of Babel?

Sophia

Age 8

Answer:

And they said, "Come, let us build ourselves a city, and a tower whose top is in the heavens..." (Genesis 11:4).

As far as we know, there was nothing inside the tower. It makes more sense that it would have been solid bricks inside, just like a ziggurat tower you might build of stacked wooden blocks.

But the Tower of Babel did have various level areas on various stories. In the last question, we read that a historian named Herodotus (who had said he had seen the old tower before it was torn down) said that there were seats about halfway up for people to rest.

On the very top of the Tower was the special place. It likely held a little structure as the top or "head" of the Tower. This was long gone by Nebuchadnezzar's day (over 1,500 years later!). He wrote that the head was not "complete."

But Jewish sources called the "Midrash" say the top had been burned. This makes sense because Nebuchadnezzar pointed out that lighting and earthquakes had done damage to the tower. Lighting usually strikes the tallest structure in the area and often starts fires. So if that top structure was struck by lightning, it makes sense that it could have burned and was long gone 1,500 years later when Nebuchadnezzar mentioned it.

Job 15:28; Judges 9:52;
Acts 7:49

Question: Why was Babel made?

Caleb

Age 5

20

Answer:

... let us make a name for ourselves, lest we be scattered abroad over the face of the whole earth" (Genesis 11:4).

The tower and city that the people built at Babel were made because they were disobeying what God had told them to do — to move over the earth. They were sinning against God — and possibly going so far as to worship the heavens instead of God.

In Genesis 9:1, God told Noah and his family something very important. Noah's family came off the ark into the new world and God said, "Be fruitful and multiply, and fill the earth."

God repeated this just a few moments later in Genesis 9:7. God said, "And as for you, be fruitful and multiply; bring forth abundantly in the earth and multiply in it."

This was important because there was no one in the world except them. God wanted them to fill the earth and take possession of it, but Noah's descendants decided to disobey God. Instead, they built a city and tower so that they would not be scattered across the earth. We read about this in Genesis 11:4.

God was very patient with them. But finally He confused their language to force them to spread out over the earth (Genesis 11:7–8). This should be a reminder to us — we should always listen to what God says in His Word, the Bible.

Genesis 9:1; Genesis 11:4; Genesis 1:7–8

21

Question:

If everyone would have scattered like God said, would there still be one language?

Neva

Age 8

22

Answer:

Therefore its name is called Babel, because there the LORD confused the language of all the earth; and from there the LORD scattered them abroad over the face of all the earth (Genesis 11:9).

Yes! There was originally only one language, so if everyone had scattered over the earth, they would have continued to speak that language. It is possible that we would have various dialects as people lived in different parts of the world — we even see that today with Canadian English, Australian English, American English, and so on. God created one language when He created Adam and Eve, so there would have been one language from Adam to Noah, when the Flood occurred. By giving families different languages at the Tower of Babel, God was making it harder for people to get together to rebel against Him. Now because of the many languages, it is important to take the message of the gospel to people groups around the world by translating His Word into those languages.

Before the Bible was completed, God provided a special event in Jerusalem so people with different languages could hear the gospel. In Acts 2, at Pentecost, God sent the Holy Spirit to come upon the Apostles to enable them to speak in many different languages. This enabled foreign people who were there to hear the good news about Jesus.

Acts 2:1–6

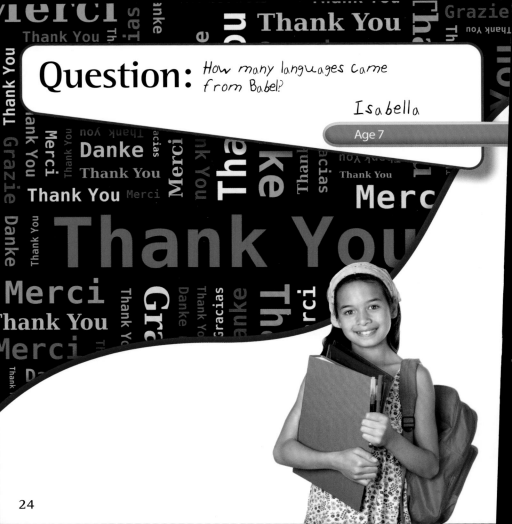

Question: How many languages came from Babel?

Isabella

Age 7

24

Answer:

And the LORD said, "Indeed the people are one and they all have one language, and this is what they begin to do; now nothing that they propose to do will be withheld from them (Genesis 11:6).

There were at least 78 families that came out of Babel with new languages because Genesis 10 gives a listing of most of these families.

We left off Noah and his three sons since they are not listed in Genesis 10 as having been divided (Genesis 10:32). We also left off Peleg as he was probably just born or very young and kept the language of his parents, since the language division occurred "in the days of Peleg" (Genesis 10:25).

Some people in Genesis 10 were intentionally left out so that they could be discussed in Genesis 11. For example, Selah had other sons and daughters in Genesis 11:14. So that means there were a minimum of 78 language families and possibly a few more. Now these language families gave rise to almost all of the languages we have today. German, English, Norwegian, Danish, Swedish, and Austrian are all part of one language family. Latin, Italian, Spanish, French, Portuguese, and Romanian are all part of another language family. If you tally these language families up around the world, there are less than 100 language families in the world today. This is a good confirmation of what the Bible says about the origin of languages at the Tower of Babel!

Genesis 10:32; Genesis 11:13–14

25

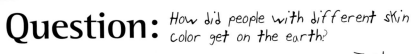

Question: How did people with different skin color get on the earth?

Zachary

Age 10

26

Answer:

Can the Ethiopian change his skin or the leopard its spots? Then may you also do good who are accustomed to do evil (Jeremiah 13:23).

Many people are under the misconception that there are different skin "colors," like red, black, white, yellow, and so on. But really, we all have the same basic skin color, from the main pigment in our skin called "melanin." This pigment is a brown color. This means that humans are all brown in color but they have different shades from dark to light.

Those people who have a lot of the brown melanin in their skin are usually called black — but they are really dark brown, not black. Those that have much less brown melanin in their skin are usually called white — but they are not white but light brown. Most people in the world are a middle brown shade. If Adam and Eve were both in the middle (middle brown) then they could have had children with dark brown skin and children with very light brown skin in one generation!

As the population split up and people left Babel by their family groups, different characteristics like the many skin shades ended up in the various groups. Some groups ended up with only dark skin, while others ended up with a light shade of skin — and others with all sorts of shades in between. What skin tone do you have?

Genesis 11:9; Acts 17:26;
John 3:16

HOLY
BIBLE

27

Question: When people spread out, how did they make it to America?

Jackson

Age 9

28

Answer:

. . . and from there the LORD scattered them abroad over the face of all the earth (Genesis 11:9).

As people spread out from Babel, many of them could have walked or ridden on animals. They could easily have made it to Europe, Asia, and Africa. These continents are all connected.

But North and South America and Australia are not connected — at least not today. After the Flood, the Ice Age occurred. This event was caused by a lot of evaporation from the then-warmer oceans, and then massive snow falls on the land where it was cooler. This caused the ocean levels to be lowered by as much as 350 feet.

This would have opened up land bridges to places like North America, so that people could walk across. It also would have opened up bridges to England, Japan, and maybe even Australia. So it is possible that people and animals walked all the way to the Americas.

But let's not forget that Noah and his sons were also able to build a great ship called the ark. Many of Noah's descendants surely learned this art of shipbuilding, too. Some of Noah's descendants were even called "coastline" or "maritime" people who traveled by boat (Genesis 10:5). Many could have come to the Americas (and other places) by boats!

Genesis 6:14; Genesis 6:22;
Genesis 10:5

Question: Where did the Chinese people come from?

Ethan
Age 6

30

Answer:

Surely these shall come from afar; Look! Those from the north and the west, and these from the land of Sinim" (Isaiah 49:12).

All people today came out of Babel (Genesis 10:32), including the Chinese people. The Chinese came from the line of Noah's son Ham and grandson Canaan. Some of these descendants were called Canaanites. One group of Canaanites was called the Sinites (Genesis 10:15–17). Like the Sinai Peninsula, the names in the area reflect the names of Sineus or the Sinites, such as Mt. Sinai where Moses received the Ten Commandments (Exodus 34:29) when leaving Egypt.

The Chinese are descendants of these original Sinites and most call themselves "Han," from Ham, one of Noah's three sons. China in ancient times was called the land of the Sinites. This name is still used and the Bible even calls this distant land the land of Sinim (Isaiah 49:12). Not all people in China are Sinites though. There are several people groups that made it to China. One group, the Maio people, have their ancestry through Noah's son Japheth and his son Gomer. But let's remember that all people in the world are descendants of Adam — which is why all people are sinners in need of salvation through Christ.

Genesis 10:15–17; Isaiah 49:12

Question: Where do the English people come from?

Grant

Age 7

32

Answer:

The sons of Gomer were Ashkenaz, Riphath, and Togarmah (Genesis 10:3).

Many Americans, Australians, Canadians, and others are descendants of the English. The English live on a quite small island off the coast of mainland Europe, but they have a lot of fascinating history. Most of the English came from Germanic tribes of the northern part of mainland Europe, namely the Angles and Saxons. "Angles" is where we get the name English from (think "Anglish").

The Germanic tribes gave rise to many of the peoples of Europe, like the Swedish, Norwegians, Austrians, Germans, English, and others. The German peoples came from their ancestor Ashkenaz. Ashkenaz was the son of Gomer, the son of Japheth, the son of Noah.

Historians have a continuous record of 20 kings from King Ashkenaz until King Wolfheim Sickenger, who reigned about the same time as King Saul in Israel! Many Jews who later settled in Germanic areas like Central Europe were called "Ashkenazi Jews" and many Jews have called Germany "Ashkenaz." Some variations of the name Ashkenaz can be found in the name Scandinavia or Scandia, which is where Sweden and Norway are (think "A-scandia" or "A-scandinavia").

Jeremiah 51:27

33

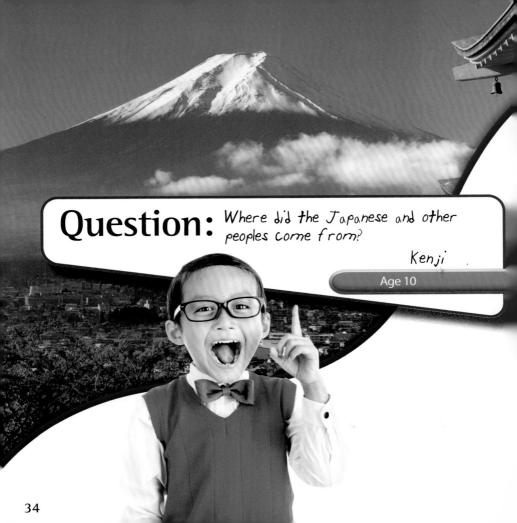

Question: Where did the Japanese and other peoples come from?

Kenji

Age 10

34

Answer:

The sons of Javan were Elishah, Tarshish, Kittim, and Dodanim (Genesis 10:4).

Many groups of people are actually descendants of more than one ancestor (although everyone is a descendant of Adam and Eve). This happened with a number of peoples, including the Japanese. A Spanish historian wrote that one of the earliest settlements on the island of Japan was by the family of Tarshish (one of Noah's great grandsons, who also inhabited one particular region of Spain), who was the son of Javan. Javan also gave rise to the Greeks, who were people who traveled by boat, so it makes sense that Tarshish would settle an island.

Several peoples invaded Japan a long time ago. Most historians think it was a mix of people from China and Mongolia. Many Japanese today are likely a mixture of some of these peoples. Here is a list of some peoples and their likely ancestry at Babel:

France: Gomer; Germany/England/Scandinavia: Ashkenaz; China: Sinites; Russia: Meshech, Tubal, Magog, Togarmah; Greece: Javan; Israelites: Arphaxad; India: Joktan, Madai, Cush; Egypt: Mizraim; Ethiopia and lower Africa: Cush. (Wow, really funny-sounding names, huh!)

Genesis 10:4–5

Question: What is the Ice Age?

Paige

Age 9

Answer:

Which are dark because of the ice, and into which the snow vanishes (Job 6:16).

The Ice Age was an event that happened after the Flood — and we believe it was generated by the Flood. At the end of the Flood, the oceans would have been warmer and the land cooler. This would have resulted in a lot of evaporation from the oceans and snow then falling on the land, resulting in a massive ice build-up on about one-third of the earth. This ice build-up would have continued for several years, causing large ice sheets and glaciers to form. Places that are naturally colder, like in the far north and the far south of earth, are the places the Ice Age affected the most. As the ice continued to build up, it pushed farther and farther into warmer areas — forming valleys.

Now evolutionary scientists think there were many ice ages over millions of years. But this isn't true. There was definitely one Ice Age several hundred years after the Flood that peaked and retreated during its duration. Since the Ice Age finally peaked, it has basically been melting and reducing ever since. But there are some places where the ice sheets are actually still growing, like in Greenland and the Antarctic Ice Cap! These places help give us an idea of what it was like when the Ice Age was growing over more of the earth.

Job 6:16–17; Job 38:22–23

HOLY BIBLE

Question: How does an Ice Age happen?

Obadiah

Age 6

38

Answer:

From whose womb comes the ice? And the frost of heaven, who gives it birth? (Job 38:29).

An ice age is a rare event. If the earth became very cold, it would not produce an ice age. It would just be a cold earth. For an ice age, we need warm oceans, cool land, and cool summers. With a warm ocean, this means more water would evaporate, resulting in more water in the air that would form more snow and ice, particularly in the wintertime. If there were cool summers, then all the snow and ice wouldn't melt off by the end of summer (warmer season). And with winter coming back each year, more snow and ice from each storm would make the layers of ice bigger and bigger. This is how an ice age starts.

During the Flood, several factors caused the oceans to heat up, such as the movement of the continents to their current positions. This would generate a lot of heat, just like rubbing your hands together very fast. Also high mountains and ranges formed as a result of these continental movements. When this happened, a lot of volcanoes erupted! Their eruptions shot very small ash particles into the upper atmosphere that lingered for many years. These ash particles reflected sunlight back to space and that cooled our planet down, especially in the summer. Warm oceans and cool summers are the key to an ice age. This is what would happen as a result of all the events associated with Noah's Flood.

Genesis 7:11; Psalm 104:8–9

39

Question: What was the extent of the Ice Age?

Noah

Age 10

40

Answer:

By the breath of God ice is given, and the broad waters are frozen (Job 37:10).

During the Ice Age, the ice extended in a downward direction from the north in Asia, Europe, and North America. It covered most of Canada, and parts of the upper United States as far down as Illinois, Indiana, and Ohio. In Europe, it extended over most of northern Europe like Sweden, Norway, and Finland, and most of England. In Asia, it covered parts of northern Russia. The ice also affected southern areas like Antarctica and stretched across the ocean almost to the southern tip of South America.

Biblical creationists (and others, even many evolutionists) agree about the extent of the ice. Where biblical creationists disagree with the secular scientists is that they think the latest ice age happened around 10,000–20,000 years ago, while we believe there was only one Ice Age and it began after the Flood, about 4,350 years ago and reached its maximum in the years following. It is possible that Job, who lived in the Middle East near the Jordan River, even saw some snow and ice that could have been associated with the time of the Ice Age. Of course, where Job lived, there was no build-up of layers into ice sheets. Most likely the snow and ice Job saw in the winter would have melted off in the summer time.

Job 6:16; Job 24:19;
Job 38:22

41

Question: Has anyone ever found a frozen person from the Ice Age?

Abram

Age 8

42

Answer:

"But not a hair of your head shall be lost" (Luke 21:18).

Believe it or not . . . they have found a man frozen in a glacier! He is named "Ötzi, the Iceman." His body was found frozen in ice in the Alps Mountains between Italy and Austria. The Alps Mountains in this area are specifically called the Ötztal Alps. This is why this frozen person is called Ötzi.

His body was found on September 19, 1991, by two German tourists named Helmut and Erika Simon. The body was still frozen, and part of it was hanging out of a glacier. At first, those who saw it thought it was someone who had recently died while hiking in the mountains.

But after further study, researchers realized it was a person from long ago, most likely during the Ice Age. Researchers suggest that Ötzi's body, which became mummified from the ice, is the oldest natural human mummy ever found in Europe.

He wore a cloak, coat, leggings, loincloth, and shoes. He even had a belt, a copper ax, a knife, and a quiver with 14 arrows in it! Ötzi stood about 5 feet, 5 inches tall (1.65 meters). Currently, Ötzi is on display in the South Tyrol Museum of Archaeology, which is in the farthest north province of Italy. And remember, Otzi was our relative — because he, like all people, was a descendant of Adam.

Hebrews 9:27; Ephesians 2:8

43

Question:

How did animals make it to America and Australia after the Flood?

Walton

Age 10

44

Answer:

Bring out with you every living thing of all flesh that is with you: birds and cattle and every creeping thing that creeps on the earth, so that they may abound on the earth, and be fruitful and multiply on the earth (Genesis 8:17).

First, flying animals could make it to all sorts of places more easily than those animals that have to walk on the land. But many people instantly think land animals couldn't have walked to Australia or North and South America from the Middle East where Noah's ark landed. But we think they could have. Actually, the event of the Ice Age is very important here. During the Ice Age, a lot of water was taken out of the oceans and accumulated on the land in the form of ice and snow. Most think that the ocean level dropped by about 350 feet! This drop would expose land bridges in different places throughout the world. Remember that Noah and his sons built the ark and it survived a global Flood! Noah lived 350 years after the Flood and Shem lived 500 years after it too. So they could easily have shared how to build some pretty neat ships. Many people could have traveled by boat to the Americas, Australia, Madagascar, and other places, possibly taking animals with them.

It makes you wonder how many animals have been taken to various parts of the world by people and we just don't have a record of it.

Genesis 9:28; Genesis 11:10–11;
Genesis 10:5

45

Question:
What kinds of animals lived in the areas affected by the Ice Age?

Eve, Jackson, and Zachary

Ages 8, 9, & 7

46

Answer:

A righteous man regards the life of his animal, but the tender mercies of the wicked are cruel (Proverbs 12:10).

The animals that lived during the Ice Age, specifically in the icy areas or more properly the areas between the ice, would be the animals that were well-equipped to handle the cold (think of furry animals) and still find food. These animals were primarily warm-blooded mammals. There were many animals that would do well, but the more famous ones were the saber-toothed cat, woolly mammoth, dire wolf, giant beaver, snowshoe hare (rabbit), mastodon, short-faced bear, musk ox, and many others like types of shrews, moles, and skunks.

Many of these have gone extinct since the Ice Age, like the saber-toothed cats, dire wolves, mastodons, and mammoths. But some have survived, like the snowshoe hares, arctic shrews, and star-nosed moles found in Minnesota and Wisconsin. At the Creation Museum, we have a replica of the third-largest and most complete skeleton of a mastodon ever found. It has flint markings on its ribs from spears and arrowheads, which help us understand that hunters were able to kill this massive creature. Man was not allowed to eat meat until after the Flood, and the Ice Age occurred after the Flood.

Genesis 1:29; Genesis 9:3; Mark 7:19

47

Answers Are Always Important!

The Bible is truly filled some amazing answers for some of our toughest faith questions. The Answers Book for Kids series answers questions from children around the world in this multi-volume series. Each volume will answer over 20 questions in a friendly and readable style appropriate for children 6–12 years old; and each covers a unique topic, including Creation and the Fall; Dinosaurs and the Flood of Noah; God and the Bible; Sin, Salvation, and the Christian Life; and more!

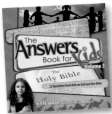

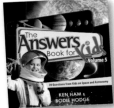

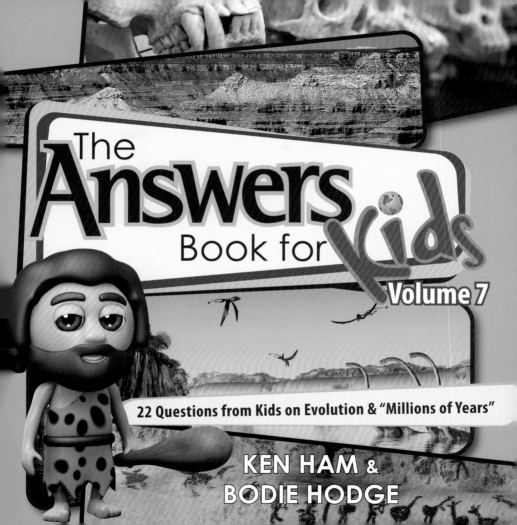

The Answers Book for Kids

Book for Kids

Volume 7

22 Questions from Kids on Evolution & "Millions of Years"

KEN HAM & BODIE HODGE

Seventh Printing: August 2022

Master Books
P.O. Box 726
Green Forest, AR 72638

Master Books® is a division of the New Leaf Publishing Group, Inc.

Printed in China

Cover and interior design by Terry White

ISBN 13: 978-1-68344-066-6
ISBN 13: 978-1-61458-630-2 (digital)

Library of Congress Control Number: 2017952422

All Scripture references are New King James Version unless otherwise noted.

Please visit our website for other great titles: www.masterbooks.com

When you see this icon, there will be related Scripture references
noted for parents to use in answering their children's, and even their
own, questions.

For Parents and Teachers

Dear parents:

The secular religions (like humanism, atheism, evolutionism) are permeating our culture. We see it in museums, media, science journals, textbooks, movies, and so much more. Even Christian kids have heard of evolution and "millions of years" (two of the tenets of secular religions) at very early ages.

As Christians, we can't hide our children and grandchildren from this religion. What we can do is teach them the truth of the Bible and the gospel, while at the same time teaching the kids why secular religions are false.

First and foremost, God disagrees with evolution and millions of years. God created in six days and this is not a problem for an all-powerful God. God made distinct kinds of animals—in other words we didn't evolve. God is to be trusted over any idea of men like evolution and millions of years. Now let's jump into some questions that kids have had on these subjects.

In Christ,

Ken and Bodie

Question: How old is the earth and universe?

Kylie

4

Answer:

In the beginning God created the heavens and the earth (Genesis 1:1).

God, who knows all things, knows how old the earth and universe are. Brilliantly, He gave us a "birth certificate" when He created them. They were created on the first day of creation.

If we add up the next 5 days, we get to the creation of Adam. He was the first man. So far, that is only 6 days. Then when we add up how old people were, like Adam and his son Seth, we can get a timeline. Adam was 130 years old when he had Seth. Then you add 105 years because that is how old Seth was when he had his son Enosh. If you keep doing this, you get about 2,000 years from Adam to Abraham.

Everyone agrees that Abraham lived about 2,000 years before Jesus, and Jesus lived about 2,000 years ago. So if you add up 6 days + 2,000 years (from Adam to Abraham) + 2,000 years (from Abraham to Christ) + 2,000 years (from Jesus until today), you get about 6,000 years. So when you start with the Bible, the earth and universe are only about 6,000 years old.

John 1:1; Exodus 20:11

Question:

Why do teachers and textbooks keep saying "millions of years ago"?

Madeline G.

Age 9

6

Answer:

Train up a child in the way he should go, and when he is old he will not depart from it (Proverbs 22:6).

In most cases, the teachers are required to say such things. This is because the state religion is secular humanism (think atheism, where man says "God does not exist"). This religion recently began to dominate the USA, England, and many other places, like France, Germany, and Australia.

When the government gives money to education or museums, they require their religion to be presented. This is why we see evolution and millions of years in state-sponsored museums like the natural history museums, state schools, and other government-funded projects.

This is why textbooks in state schools speak of millions of years and evolution. There are textbooks that do not have those things in them, but you don't find them in state-run schools. Evolution, millions of years, and the big bang are part of the religion of humanism/atheism. In the same way, six-day creation, the Fall of mankind into sin, and the Flood of Noah are a part of Christianity.

It is a battle over two different religions. Sadly, teachers are stuck in the middle of this debate.

Deuteronomy 11:19; Proverbs 9:9;
Matthew 28:19–20

Question:

Who started the idea of evolution?

Gershom & Paige

Ages 8 & 9

8

Answer:

$W = hf_0$

$P_m = \dfrac{I_m V_m}{}$

You alone are the LORD; You have made heaven, the heaven of heavens, with all their host, the earth and everything on it, the seas and all that is in them, and You preserve them all. The host of heaven worships You (Nehemiah 9:6).

Some of the first evolutionists were Greeks called the Epicureans. They lived after the Old Testament was already written! They believed things evolved from tiny particles. Paul proved them wrong in Acts 17, and this view basically died for 1,800 years.

Around 1800, a man named Jean Lamarck brought back a type of evolution called Lamarckian evolution. Then later in 1859, Charles Darwin came up with a different type of evolution based on *natural selection*. But that still didn't make evolution happen. Even some in the church began to believe in evolution.

Most evolutionists now believe in "neo-Darwinism" or "new-evolution." They say *natural selection + mutations* will lead to evolution (new and better animals and plants). But that still doesn't work when we watch things in nature. Mutations cause big problems in creatures, like defects, cancer, and missing body parts! So things are NOT getting better with mutations.

So even though a lot of people believe evolution, it still doesn't work. It is better to trust in God's Word and realize that God specially created things. This would be an easy job for an all-powerful God.

Colossians 1:16; Hebrews 1:1–2

Question:

Why do people think the earth (and everything else) came from nothing?

Eve

Age 8

10

Answer:

For since the creation of the world His invisible attributes are clearly seen, being understood by the things that are made, even His eternal power and Godhead, so that they are without excuse (Romans 1:20).

Sadly, there are people who do not like God and the Bible, so they try to invent a different history than what God teaches in His Word. They make up a story to try to satisfy their understanding of the past.

By doing this, the people are ignoring what really happened at creation. This is called "suppressing the truth." God says that when they do this, they have no excuse.

Since some people do not want all things to come from God, then from where do things come? Believe it or not, they have little choice but to say that "all things come from nothing" — all by themselves!

It sounds crazy, doesn't it? We don't see things coming from nothing. But this is what some people have to believe in order to reject God. This "suppression of the truth" should be a reminder to us that we should always trust God's Word in all subjects — especially creation — as the Lord will never be wrong.

Romans 1:18–19; Psalm 14:1

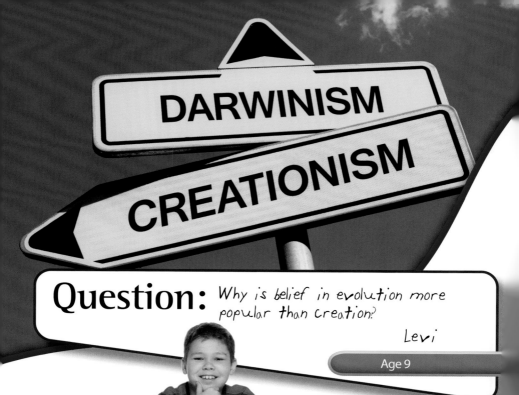

Question: Why is belief in evolution more popular than creation?

Levi

Age 9

12

Answer:

Enter by the narrow gate; for wide is the gate and broad is the way that leads to destruction, and there are many who go in by it (Matthew 7:13).

Evolution is not necessarily more popular than creation. In fact, more Americans believe creation than evolution. But in some places, it is true that evolution is more popular. One of those places is England, where Charles Darwin, the founder of modern evolution, lived. Broad (large) is the path to destruction in England right now!

Sadly, the governments of many places like England and the United States impose the religion of evolution on many kids. We see this in state schools and state-funded museums.

We also see this influence of evolution by media (news people for example) who believe in evolution. We even see it in many movies — especially kid movies! Even many Disney® movies, which are geared toward families, have evolution in them.

As Christians, we need to recognize that this religion of evolution is a *false* religion and God's Word is true. We need to be on lookout for this religion so we can spot it and not be deceived by it.

2 Timothy 3:13; James 1:16

Question: How did people get the idea that we evolved from fish, frogs, and "apemen"?

Nancy K.

Age 8

14

Answer:

Professing to be wise, they became fools, and changed the glory of the incorruptible God into an image made like corruptible man — and birds and four-footed animals and creeping things (Romans 1:22–23).

There are two reasons evolutionists believe we evolved from "lower life forms." First, evolutionists think that all things evolved from a simple, singled-celled organism (or something like it) — similar to an amoeba. By the way, these single-celled organisms are not simple, but complex little biological factories!

Evolutionists believe that this amoeba-like creature had to evolve into higher organisms until man. But we don't observe this, so it is not science, but a story like a fairy tale.

The second reason is due to the rock layers that have fossils. Evolutionists believe the rocks were formed slowly over millions of years. They believe each layer was a time period a long time ago. The rock layers have sea creatures, then amphibians, then reptiles, and lastly mammals (there are many exceptions to this, by the way). So they assume that man had to evolve through what was buried in each layer.

However, most of those rock layers were laid down during the Flood of Noah, and it is an order of burial. Sea creatures were first since they live in the ocean; then amphibians and reptiles, which sink when they die; and finally, mammals, which tend to float.

Luke 17:27; Titus 1:14

15

Question:

Where did the idea of millions of years come from?

Kylie

Age 6

Answer:

And the waters prevailed exceedingly on the earth, and all the high hills under the whole heaven were covered (Genesis 7:19).

As we talked about earlier, a few Greeks believed in an infinite (never ending) past, and the Apostle Paul argues against them in Acts 17. Nobody really believes that anymore. But very few believed in millions of years until about 200 years ago.

People who did not respect God and the Bible said that we should leave out the Bible when we discuss how old the earth is. Scientists started guessing how old the earth was by looking at rock layers. They ignored the Bible's account of the Flood, and assumed the rock layers were laid down slowly over millions of years.

A man named Charles Lyell said the rock layers were evidence of slow build-up of dirt and rock over "millions of years." Lyell said there was no global Flood. Of course, God disagrees with Lyell because God said a Flood covered everything under the heavens. The Flood makes more sense of the rock layers.

But many people were tricked into thinking Lyell was right and that God was wrong. Today, we still have to deal with people falsely believing in millions of years instead of a global Flood.

Genesis 7:20–23

LIES

uninstalling . . .

Question: Why did people start believing in evolution?

Sergio K.

Age 10

Answer:

For if you believed Moses, you would believe Me; for he wrote about Me. But if you do not believe his writings, how will you believe My words? (John 5:46–47).

It is the same reason people start to follow after other false religions — they don't want to follow God and His Word. Sadly, there are many people who don't want to be accountable to God and the Bible. Therefore, they want to give reasons for their unbelief. So they try to reject and ignore the knowledge of God. This means they are willing to believe anything else — including evolution — instead of Genesis.

When evolution began gaining popularity in the 1800s, it gave people an alternative to believing in creation. Many early evolutionists felt like they had a good reason for rejecting God. What they didn't realize was that they are just buying into a false story about the past instead of the truth.

Evolutionists were rejecting Genesis (written by Moses), which explains the foundation of sin. It was Adam's sin that brought death and suffering into the world. Jesus Christ, the Son of God, stepped into history to become a man and die on the Cross. It was Christ taking our punishment that made salvation possible.

Without the creation-gospel message, life is meaningless and hopeless. That is the "fruit" of an evolutionary worldview.

Psalm 119:118; John 14:6

19

Question:

If evolutionists say that dinosaurs evolved into birds, how do they explain birds being here, especially if all the dinosaurs became extinct at the same time from a meteorite that hit earth?

Joy B.

Age Unknown

20

Answer:

Do not be deceived, my beloved brethren (James 1:16).

The problem here is that different evolutionists believe different things and they don't agree with each other. Some believe the story that dinosaurs turned into birds.

Other evolutionists believe the story about a meteorite (comet/"impactor") that struck the earth and killed the dinosaurs. But these are two different models. Do not be deceived — both of these views are wrong, because God told the true account of history in Genesis 1.

There is evidence of a Theropod dinosaur that ate three birds,[1] so birds and dinosaurs (land animals) were living at the same time — as we expect from six-day creation (Genesis 1:21–25).

The reason dinosaurs have died out is due to sin. With sin in Genesis 3, things began to die and some animals, not just dinosaurs, have gone extinct.

The dinosaur bones we find in the fossil layers are primarily from Noah's Flood. Dinosaurs have died out since the time of the Flood, just like many other animals like dodo birds, saber-toothed cats, and mammoths.

Genesis 7:22; Exodus 23:1

Question: Did "cave men" exist?

Annie

Age 10

22

Answer:

And there he went into a cave, and spent the night in that place; and behold, the word of the LORD came to him, and He said to him, "What are you doing here, Elijah?" (1 Kings 19:9).

I presume this is meant to refer to "missing links" between man and ape-like creatures. In that case, no. Missing links are not going to be found. There are no step-by-step ape-to-human intermediates.

People keep trying to make them though. There are three ways they do this. They take an ape and try to make it look human when they draw it or make a model of it for a museum. This is the case of a famous one called Lucy. Lucy was just an ape, but evolutionists try to make it look human.

The second way is to take a human and make it look like an ape. This is what evolutionists have done with Neanderthals. Neanderthals are human, but they make them look like an intermediate between apes and humans in images and museum models.

The last way evolutionists try to make a missing link is to fake it. This happened with Piltdown man. But people are getting better at fakes, so beware! God made humans and apes distinct on day 6 of creation.

Genesis 1:24–28

23

Question:

Were the continents ever connected?

Annie

Age 10

24

Answer:

Then God said, "Let the waters under the heavens be gathered together into one place, and let the dry land appear"; and it was so (Genesis 1:9).

Most creationists believe there was just one continent in the beginning. They get this from Genesis 1:9. All the water was in one place, so we assume the land was too. Naturally, we cannot be absolutely sure of this, but it seems like a good idea.

Today, we have seven continents. So how did that happen? The evolutionists believe that it happened slowly, with millions of years of slow, gradual movements. Keep in mind this is not science, because science is observable and repeatable.

Creationists believe that the Flood of Noah's day (Genesis 6–8) is what caused the breakup and splitting into the continents of today. The mountains of Ararat (that Noah's Ark landed in) were pushed up as a result of continental collision. Much of the continental movement was done by that stage of the Flood.

It comes down to trusting what God says happened in the past versus the stories that people who oppose God make up about the past. God is never wrong, but imperfect people are wrong about the past far too often.

Genesis 7:11, 8:2

THEORY

REALITY

Question: Why do evolutionists keep believing when there is proof it isn't true?

Becca

Age 9

Answer:

Take heed to yourselves, lest your heart be deceived, and you turn aside and serve other gods and worship them (Deuteronomy 11:16).

We do not observe the biological changes necessary for evolution. We do not have the billions of missing links that are supposed to be there. It doesn't take millions of years to make oil, coal, petrified wood, rock layers, fossils, canyons, and so on. Without millions of years, there can be no evolution.

People often believe things that they know are not true. Romans 1 shows that people are without excuse, knowing in their hearts (heart often means mind in the Bible) that God created the world. God points out that people "try to hide" this knowledge.

They deceived themselves into believing evolution, and they worship evolution as the truth. The Bible speaks of this unrighteous deception:

And for this reason God will send them strong delusion, that they should believe the lie, that they all may be condemned who did not believe the truth but had pleasure in unrighteousness (2 Thessalonians 2:11–12).

The unrighteous want to be deceived; God permitted them to be deluded by a lie. Unless they repent, they will be judged.

Romans 1:18–21

27

Question:

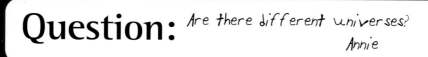

Are there different universes?

Annie

Age 10

Answer:

In the beginning God created the heavens and the earth (Genesis 1:1).

A multiverse is an idea that there are multiple universes all coexisting at the same time. You need to understand that this is just a strange suggestion (hypothesis) that has no basis in reality.

Based on the Bible, there are good reasons that a multiverse is false anyway. For example, one reason that a few people believe in a multiverse is to downplay our own universe to say ours is not special. However, God created the universe (with phrases like "heavens and earth"). It was specially created, and the earth was specifically designed for life.

For those holding to a multiverse, they presume there was no God and that everything came from nothing, has no purpose, and nothing is special — not even the earth or our universe. So to pretend our universe is not special, they make up a story to say there are a whole lot of universes and ours is just one of many!

God specially created the universe, earth, and man. And Jesus, the Son of God, became a man to save us right here *on this earth in this universe.* That is indeed special!

Isaiah 45:18; 2 Peter 3:10–13

29

Question: Why did they name the ape "Lucy"?

Eve

Age 8

30

Answer:

So God created man in His own image; in the image of God He created him; male and female He created them (Genesis 1:27).

Lucy was an ape whose fossils were found in Ethiopia in eastern Africa. Lucy's fossil is officially named AL 288-1.

When researchers found the fossils in 1974, there was a song called "Lucy in the Sky with Diamonds," from a famous band called the Beatles. This song was played over and over again in their camp. So they nicknamed the fossils . . . Lucy.

Lucy was found in rock layers that came after the Flood (post-Flood sediment). So Lucy lived after Noah and the Flood. In other words Adam, Eve, and Noah all lived before Lucy, so clearly Lucy isn't a missing link between apes and humans!

Many evolutionists take Lucy and draw it to look "half-human" and "half-ape" because they really want this to be a missing link. We even see artists do this with Lucy in museums too.

However, with an honest look at the fossils, Lucy is just an ape. Its bone measurements are very similar to a chimpanzee. So it is really just a type of chimp that existed post-Flood. This is what we expect — humans are humans and apes are apes.

Genesis 6:20; 1 Corinthians 15:39

31

Question:
Why doesn't God make the evolutionists extinct?

Emma

Age 8

32

Answer:

The Lord is not slack concerning His promise, as some count slackness, but is longsuffering toward us, not willing that any should perish but that all should come to repentance (2 Peter 3:9).

Be kind! Did you know that all of us fall short of the glory of God (Romans 3:23)? In fact, evolution is just one of many false ideas, but the Lord is patient with us.

God wants evolutionists (and anyone in false religions) to repent and come to know the truth in the Bible. *Repent* means to turn from, and be sorry for sin and false beliefs. God is patient (longsuffering) about this too.

There have been many false religions throughout history, many of which no longer exist. Some false views last longer than others. God's religion, Christianity, will last and the others will eventually fade. The Bible says the Church will prevail (Matthew 16:18). Ultimately, all false worldviews will finally "go extinct" when God creates a new heavens and new earth.

Sometimes we don't understand why God is so patient, but it is comforting to know that God knows what He is doing.

Matthew 16:18; Revelation 21:1, 27

HOLY BIBLE

Question: Are some people more evolved than others like different skin tones?

Audrey

Age 10

Answer:

And He [God] has made from one blood every nation of men to dwell on all the face of the earth, and has determined their preappointed times and the boundaries of their dwellings (Acts 17:26).

This is a common evolutionary teaching that began with people like Charles Darwin and Ernst Haeckel (a German evolutionist in the 1800s). They taught that as people evolved from apes, some people were more evolved and others were less evolved. Darwin was sure that the "more evolved" race would kill all the other races, as he noted in his book *The Descent of Man*.

The Bible shows that all people are descendants of Adam and Eve, who were our first parents created by God. There is only one race — the human race — or as some people say "Adam's race."

In the New Testament Paul agreed that we are all related when he said all people were from "one blood." We do have variation in our skin tone, but we are basically all a shade of brown (based primarily on our brownish skin pigment called *melanin*), so we are not really red, yellow, black, and white!

Because we are all related, we are all sinners and in need of Jesus Christ no matter what we look like.

Genesis 3:20; 1 Corinthians 15:45

HOLY BIBLE

Question: Did God stop creating, or is He still creating today?

J.R.

Age unknown

36

Answer:

For behold, I create new heavens and a new earth; and the former shall not be remembered or come to mind (Isaiah 65:17).

Creation week is over. God is no longer creating in the way that He did back then. In fact, God rested on the seventh day (called the Sabbath day) and instituted rest. This is why a seven-day week exists.

God didn't need to rest, but He did this as a pattern for us — the Sabbath day of rest was made for man, not man for the Sabbath (Mark 2:27). Just because God rested doesn't mean He is not active in His creation.

God still performed miraculous creations after creation week. For instance, Jesus created wine from water and food for 5,000 people. Also, Christians, as fallen and sinful people, are created new (Psalm 51:10). Second Corinthians 5:17 says:

Therefore, if anyone is in Christ, he is a new creation; old things have passed away; behold, all things have become new.

The Bible points out that when Jesus ascended into heaven, He went away to prepare a place for us. Yes, God is still active, and creating things is an easy task for an all-powerful God — who can do all His holy will.

John 14:2–3; Hebrews 1:3;
Revelation 4:11

Question: Why are there still apes if we supposedly evolved from apes?

Grace

Age 11

38

Answer:

Test all things; hold fast what is good (1 Thessalonians 5:21).

There is a problem right from the start. There is the confusion over the word "ape." Allow me to explain it like this: Why are there still *modern apes like gorillas and chimpanzees* if we supposedly evolved from *ancient ape-like creatures that we call apes*?

The problem is that we called this alleged ape-like ancestor... an ape. The evolutionists believe this ape-like ancestor gave rise to modern apes — like the chimps and gorillas — but also gave rise to man. So evolutionists still expect modern apes to exist, even within their story.

The big problem is with *the evolutionary story*. When we test this story against the Bible, it fails. There are no ancient ape-like creatures long before apes and man. Both man and apes were made on the 6th day of creation.

What we find in the fossil record are apes and humans. Ape and human fossils are found in post-Flood rock (though it is possible that some could be found in Flood rock). The point is that Noah (and his family) and the two apes with him on the ark existed before these fossils were formed. Modern apes are descendants of the two that were on the ark.

Genesis 8:1; Ephesians 5:6;
Colossians 2:4

39

Question: Do all scientists believe in evolution?

Noah

Age 9

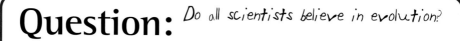

Answer:

Teach me good judgment and knowledge, for I believe Your commandments (Psalm 119:66).

I (Bodie) am a scientist. I worked and taught in science for years developing new technology (materials and engineering). I do not believe in evolution. There are many scientists who believe evolution and there are many who do not. I know of thousands who do not believe in evolution.

Most fields of science ("knowledge") were actually developed by Bible-believing Christians. These include Isaac Newton (who was arguably the greatest scientist to ever live), Robert Boyle, Johannes Kepler, Galileo Galilei, Louis Pasteur, Gregor Mendel, and many more.

There are modern scientists who are Bible-believers too. For example there is Dr. Raymond Damadian, who invented a medical machine called an MRI. There is Dr. Jason Lisle (astrophysicist), Dr. Andrew Snelling (geologist), Dr. Danny Faulkner (astronomer), Dr. Tommy Mitchell (medical doctor), Dr. David Menton (anatomist), Dr. Georgia Purdom and Dr. Nathaniel Jeanson (geneticists), Dr. Stuart Burgess (engineer), Dr. David DeWitt (neuroscience), and many others.

Creationists recognize that God upholds all things in a consistent way. This is what makes observable and repeatable science possible. When we study God's creation using science, we like to say, as Kepler did, that we are "thinking God's thoughts after Him."

Proverbs 1:5, 17:24

41

Question:

Why do evolutionists believe in big bang?

Annie

Age 10

42

Answer:

By faith we understand that the worlds were framed by the word of God, so that the things which are seen were not made of things which are visible (Hebrews 11:3).

Evolution is built on the idea that there is no God who created in the past. All things had to come from somewhere, but evolutionists don't want God involved. So if God didn't create everything, then the only other option is to say things came about by themselves, without God.

This is what big bang is. It is a religious belief about origins that says there was nothing . . . then something popped into existence from nothing. This "cosmic egg" or "singularity" then rapidly expanded (exploded) and finally arrived at what we have today.

Keep in mind that no one has ever observed this and no one could recreate it. It is not science, but just a story (a myth) that some people came up with because they didn't want to trust what God says.

Sadly, some Christians try to add the big-bang myth to the Bible and say that God started the big bang. But this doesn't make sense, because God would NOT have created anything if the big bang happened. There is no reason to add this false story of the big bang to the Bible.

Nehemiah 9:6; Romans 12:2

43

Question: Do any evolutionists believe God is real, and is it okay to mix Christianity with evolution?

Neva & Reens

Age 10

44

Answer:

Do not be deceived, God is not mocked; for whatever a man sows, that he will also reap (Galatians 6:7).

They are generally called "theistic evolutionists." Theistic means they believe in God. Basically, some Christians reject God's Word in Genesis and adopt the evolutionary story instead. This is inconsistent (not a good way to think).

What they are doing is mixing their Christianity with the religion of evolution, which is part of the religion of humanism/atheism.

In the Old Testament, godly Israelites started to worship "false gods" along with the true God. It was inconsistent for them to worship the true God, and then turn around and worship false gods. God was angry at the Israelites and judged them harshly!

Even the very wise and smart King Solomon began worshiping false gods. The Lord was angry with King Solomon too. Do you think God is angry when Christians mix their religion with false religions like humanism and evolution?

Christians should believe what God said about creation instead of believing evolution. God was there, and He knows what happened. There is no reason to trade what God said in Genesis for the false religion of evolution.

1 Kings 9:6–9

45

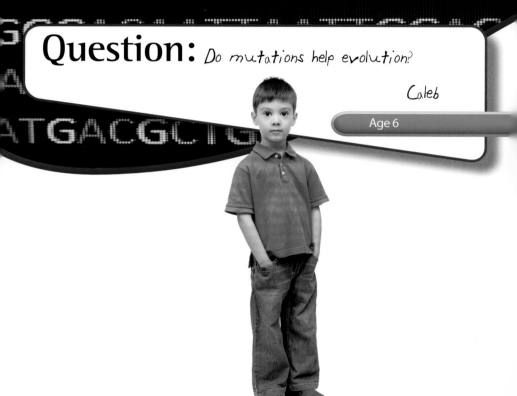

Question: Do mutations help evolution?

Caleb

Age 6

46

Answer:

His parents answered them and said, "We know that this is our son, and that he was born blind" (John 9:20).

Mutations are mistakes in your DNA (the code that builds your body). They can cause serious diseases or cause people to have problems with their arms, legs, or other parts of their body — like being born blind!

Evolution teaches that a single-celled organism — like an amoeba — changed (by mutation) into all the animals that we have today. For the "amoeba" to change into a dog (over long ages), it would have to mutate the DNA to get information for hair, eyes, lungs, nerves, blood, and so on. But mutations don't produce things like this.

Instead, mutations actually cause big problems. Mutations create problems that cause the animal to be broken. They are hailed as the hero for evolution, but mutations actually destroy animals and cause big problems.

Mutations are real, but they are problems that are not helpful. Mutations are part of a broken world that happened as a result of sin in Genesis 3. In heaven, we won't have to worry about this anymore.

2 Samuel 21:20; Revelation 21:4

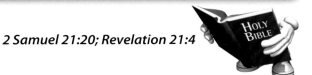

47

Answers Are Always Important!

The Bible is truly filled some amazing answers for some of our toughest faith questions. The Answers Book for Kids series answers questions from children around the world in this multi-volume series. Each volume will answer over 20 questions in a friendly and readable style appropriate for children 6–12 years old; and each covers a unique topic, including Creation and the Fall; Dinosaurs and the Flood of Noah; God and the Bible; Sin, Salvation, and the Christian Life; and more!

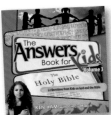

Endnote
[1] L. Xing, P. Bell, W. Persons, S. Ji, T. Miyashita, et al., Abdominal Contents from Two Large Early Cretaceous Compsognathids (Dinosauria: Theropoda) Demonstrate Feeding on Confuciusornithids and Dromaeosaurids, PLoS ONE 7(8): e44012. doi:10.1371/journal.pone.0044012, August 29, 2012.

The Answers Book for Kids

Volume 8

22 Questions from Kids on Satan & Angels

KEN HAM & BODIE HODGE

Seventh Printing: August 2022

Master Books
P.O. Box 726
Green Forest, AR 72638

Master Books® is a division of the New Leaf Publishing Group, Inc.

Printed in China

Cover and interior design by Terry White

ISBN 13: 978-1-68344-067-3
ISBN 13: 978-1-61458-631-9 (digital)

Library of Congress Control Number: 2017952419

All Scripture references are New King James Version unless otherwise noted.

Please visit our website for other great titles: www.masterbooks.com

When you see this icon, there will be related Scripture references noted for parents to use in answering their children's, and even their own, questions.

For Parents and Teachers

Dear parents:

As we dive into this final book of the series, let's reflect on the previous books' questions. There were multitudes of them! Kids have a lot of questions and this is a good thing. So we really need to be diligent in giving them biblical answers.

Regardless of the questions children may ask, we want to encourage you to open the Bible and search for the correct answer. This is what we love to do. And our hope is that you will have that same love for truth of the Bible. God's Word is always true and this is something in which we can rest assured.

When it comes to Satan and angels, God is our only reliable source of information. Are you ready to see the questions we received from the kids? Here we go!

Blessings in Christ,

Ken and Bodie

Question: Is there one angel or many, and do we know any of their names?

Tyler and Isabella

Ages 10 & 7

4

Answer:

Or do you think that I [Jesus] cannot now pray to My Father, and He will provide Me with more than twelve legions of angels? (Matthew 26:53).

God is our only reliable source of information about angels. In the Bible, angel means "messenger," and they are spirits (Hebrews 1:14). This means they do not have bodies like we do.

There are many angels, and Jesus tells us about legions of them. A legion was usually no less than about 6,000 soldiers. Jesus gave us a clue that at least 72,000 angels were at His command for this one instance if He wanted them. The point is that there are a lot of angels. There were different types of messengers (angels) in the Bible. In some cases, even the Lord was the messenger, being the *Angel of the Lord* (Genesis 16:7–13).

The Bible reveals only two names of angels. One of them was Michael — a chief angel, which is also called an "archangel." He was chief over a group of other angels (Jude 1:9; Revelation 12:7).

Another angel was Gabriel. He helped Daniel understand his vision in the Old Testament. He was also the angel who brought good news to Mary that she was to be the mother of baby Jesus. Sometimes, people have suggested names for other angels, but these names do not come from the Bible.

*Luke 1:19; Jude 1:9;
Revelation 12:7*

Question: Do angels have halos and wings?

Becca and Ethan

Ages 9 & 4

Answer:

One wing of the cherub was five cubits, and the other wing of the cherub five cubits: ten cubits from the tip of one wing to the tip of the other (1 Kings 6:24).

The Bible doesn't mention halos. There is much history about the halo both from Christian and non-Christian sources. When dealing with halo art, Christians usually view it as symbolizing the "light of the world" and "crown of glory" that shines from Christ, Christians, and angels. Again, this has to do with art, not necessarily reality.

Angelic beings, like the ones in our verse, can also be called a cherub or cherubim (plural). Even though angels are spiritual beings, God describes the cherubim as having wings and hands.

A nice description of cherubim is given in the Bible. They were to be figurines on the "Ark of the Covenant," also called the "Ark of the Testimony," which held the Ten Commandments (it was a fancy box!). Their wings extended over the "mercy seat," which was like a lid that sat on top of the Ark of the Covenant.

God also placed cherubim at the entrance to the Garden of Eden to keep man from returning to the Tree of Life in Genesis 3. This was after Adam and Eve sinned and were kicked out of the Garden. These cherubim were armed with flaming swords!

Exodus 25:20; Ezekiel 10:8

HOLY BIBLE

7

Question:

What do angels do besides singing?

Tyler & Becca

Ages 10 & 9

Answer:

Praise Him, all His angels; praise Him, all His hosts! (Psalm 148:2).

Angels are ministering spirits (Hebrews 1:14). Therefore, they minister (preach)! After Jesus was temped by Satan, angels came and ministered to Jesus (Matthew 4:11).

Angels also do other things, like giving messages. This was the case with Gabriel giving Mary the message that she would be the mother of Jesus (Luke 1:26–38). An angel gave messages to Elijah too (2 Kings 1:3).

Another thing angels did was to enact judgment and fight in war (e.g., 2 Chronicles 32:21; Revelation 12:7). Angels also praise God (Psalm 148:2). When Jesus was born, hosts of heavenly beings (which included angels) praised God (Luke 2:13). These are just a few of the tasks that God created angels to perform.

Interestingly, there is something that angels do not do. Angels do not get married! Jesus mentioned this in Matthew 22:30. Also, we are not to pray to angels since Jesus is our only mediator ("go between") to God (1 Timothy 2:5). We are not to worship angels either since God alone is to be worshiped (Revelation 19:10, 22:8–9).

Hebrews 1:13–14; 2 Samuel 24:16; 1 Kings 1:15

9

Question:

If Satan was an angel and turned bad, does that mean there are other bad angels?

Jaden

Age unknown

10

Answer:

So the great dragon was cast out, that serpent of old, called the Devil and Satan, who deceives the whole world; he was cast to the earth, and his angels were cast out with him (Revelation 12:9).

The Bible describes Satan (who is also called the devil, great dragon, or Lucifer) as being among the heavenly host. He was also called a cherub (Ezekiel 28:14), so this means he could be called a type of angel.

When Satan fell, it was due to his pride to ascend above God to be God. Originally, Satan was created perfect, like all of creation (Genesis 1:31; Deuteronomy 32:4), but when sin was found in him, he was cast out.

The Bible says in Revelation 12:7: "And war broke out in heaven: Michael [*an archangel*] and his angels fought with the dragon [Satan]; and the dragon and his angels fought."

When Satan rebelled and his angels with him, they were all cast out of heaven. Sometimes, angels were "*metaphorically*" equated with stars or "*luminaries*" (things that shine in the sky). In Revelation 12:3–4, Satan (the great dragon) caused one-third of the stars (angels) to fall from heaven. The bad angels are often equated with demons now.

When it comes down to it, Satan and his angels (who are all created beings) have no power next to the all-powerful Creator God.

2 Peter 2:4; Jude 1:6

11

Question: Why did God create the devil when He knew that he would turn against Him and against people too?

Reese and Sarah

Ages 9 & 7

12

Answer:

He who sins is of the devil, for the devil has sinned from the beginning. For this purpose the Son of God was manifested, that He might destroy the works of the devil (1 John 3:8).

God always had a plan, and God always knew what would happen. God knows all things, so Satan's rebellion was not a "surprise" to God (Psalm 147:5).

God's plan works in spite of Satan's sin and rebellion. God can use all things to work for the good of those who love Him (Romans 8:28). When Satan sinned, and then used a serpent to deceive Eve (and then Adam) into sin (Genesis 3), God already had a plan in place to rescue sinners through His Son Jesus (Genesis 3:15).

The Bible says that Jesus (the Lamb) was slain from the beginning (Revelation 13:8). This means that God always knew Satan would sin and lead man into rebellion. Christ had a plan to lay down His life for those who love God, and take His life back up again (John 10:17–18).

Satan only has a little time to deceive man, and then his time is up. He will be cast into the "lake of fire" or "hell" forever, which was prepared for him (Matthew 25:41). Then those who love Christ, who is God, will live eternally without sin, death, or Satan to destroy things.

Matthew 25:41; Romans 8:28

Question: Why did Satan lie to Eve?

Zachary

Age 6

14

Answer:

We know that we are of God, and the whole world lies under the sway of the wicked one (1 John 5:19).

When Satan sinned, he decided to go after God's most prized creation — mankind. Satan was created during creation week (like all other created things — Colossians 1:16). He witnessed God creating man in God's own image. He saw God give man dominion (to rule) over earth.

Satan tried to overthrow God in heaven because he wanted to rule. Satan sinned and was cast out of heaven (to earth). When Satan sinned, it only affected him as well as those angels that sinned with him.

Then Satan used a serpent for the purpose of deceiving Eve (and ultimately Adam). It wasn't by accident. Satan intentionally attacked those who ruled over the earth. Just like he tried to rule in heaven, he tried to rule on earth by tempting Eve to follow his deception instead of following God. John 8:44 says that Satan is the "father of lies."

Sadly, Eve and Adam both stumbled and disobeyed God, just like Satan wanted. So man sinned. This is why the world "lies under the sway of the wicked one." Satan attacked God — and Adam and Eve whom God loved. Today, we still see Satan attacking people that God loves.

John 8:44; 1 John 3:8

Question: Why does Satan hate God?

Zachary

Age 6

16

Answer:

But he who sins against me wrongs his own soul; all those who hate me love death (Proverbs 8:36).

God is the life (John 14:6). Satan sinned against God. This proved that he loved death more than he loved life. As Satan's love for death grew more and more, his new hate for God grew more and more. Satan is consumed with hate like a fire (Ezekiel 28:18).

Satan's hatred for God extends to man because we are made in God's image. And God loves us. So Satan is the personal adversary of both God and man. The Bible says to hate evil and love good (Amos 5:15). But Satan loves evil and hates good. All good things come from God so Satan's hatred for God extends to the good things that come from God. When people love Jesus and turn from their sin and wickedness, Satan will not like it. But Jesus said in John 15:18:

If the world hates you, you know that it hated Me before it hated you.

Jesus also said in Luke 6:27:

But I say to you who hear: Love your enemies, do good to those who hate you.

We should mimic God's good love, and not Satan's hate and evil.

John 3:20; James 4:7

Question:

Does God love Satan?

Amity

Age unknown

Answer:

He who does not love does not know God, for God is love (1 John 4:8).

Prior to Satan's sin, there would have been no reason to think that God did not love Satan. God is love (1 John 4:8). And God's "very good" creation in six days included Satan (Genesis 1:31; Exodus 20:11). So it makes sense that God indeed loved Satan.

When Satan chose disobedience (sin) against God, Satan became the father of lies, sin, and evil. Does God love these things? Not at all. God hates lying, sin, and evil (Proverbs 6:16–19), and we should be the same way (Psalm 97:10).

We should hate evil and sin. Hate can be a good or bad thing depending on what we are talking about. You should not hate your family or God or good and righteous things, but you should hate evil and sin.

Have there been examples in your life where you loved sin more than God? If so, you should repent (be sorry and turn from that sin). Satan did not repent, and he never will. God knows the future and told us that Satan will be punished forever because of his sin (Revelation 20:10). This means Satan will never repent.

Proverbs 6:16–19; Psalm 97:10

19

Question: Animals can't talk, so how could the serpent talk?

Meagan and Talia

Ages 9 & 7

20

Answer:

Now the serpent was more cunning than any beast of the field which the LORD God had made. And he said to the woman, "Has God indeed said, 'You shall not eat of every tree of the garden'?" (Genesis 3:1).

Actually, some animals, like many birds, do "talk"! But they don't make sense. For example, a blue-fronted Amazon parrot has the ability to speak. It mimics things that were already said, but a bird mimicking speech doesn't understand the meaning behind what is said.

When the serpent that was in the Garden of Eden was originally created, it obviously had an ability to speak (not sure about other serpents). Being an animal, though, it was limited in its intelligence. It could be clever, cunning, or crafty, but not like a human who is made in God's image.

When Satan influenced the serpent to speak, then it made sense to Eve (the words had meaning). It wasn't because the serpent understood language, but it was Satan speaking lies through the serpent, who was used as a "vessel."

The original serpent was cursed to crawl on its belly and eat dust as part of its new diet (Genesis 3:14). The serpent's original body was changed due to the Curse. Its ability to talk was lost. Whether all serpents originally had the ability to speak, we don't know. We know that living serpents today can't "talk."

Genesis 3:14; 2 Corinthians 11:3

21

Question: Do angels ever come down to earth?

Paige

Age 10

22

Answer:

So Jacob went on his way, and the angels of God met him (Genesis 32:1).

Besides Jacob, there are several examples in the Bible where God permitted angels to be seen and do things on earth. There were two angels that came with the Lord to rescue Lot when God destroyed some evil cities called Sodom and Gomorrah. This was in the Book of Genesis, chapter 19.

In Numbers 22:31–35, we read about an angel who confronted a man named Baalam. Even King David saw an angel (2 Samuel 24:17).

Gabriel was probably the most famous angel encounter. Gabriel was the angel who gave Mary the message that she was favored of God to bring Jesus the Messiah into the world (Luke 1:26–33).

The Bible says that some people are visited by angels and they don't even realize it! The Book of Hebrews says:

Do not forget to entertain strangers, for by so doing some have unwittingly entertained angels (Hebrews 13:2).

When angels appear to people, they look like people, but this doesn't mean they are human. People (mankind) are descendants of Adam and angels are not — they are still angels and will return to their original spiritual form.

Luke 1:26–33

23

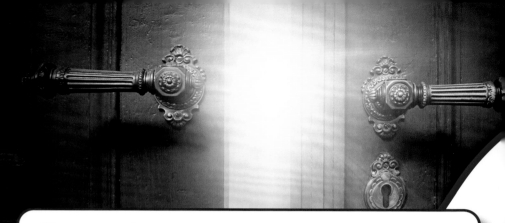

Question: What happened to Satan at the beginning?

Walton

Age 10

24

Answer:

You were perfect in your ways from the day you were created, till iniquity was found in you (Ezekiel 28:15).

Satan was originally perfect and without sin. God created things perfectly (Deuteronomy 32:4) and His creation was very good (Genesis 1:31), including Satan. He was without sin, until the day that he did sin (Ezekiel 28:15).

Satan sinned of his own desire. James 1:14–15 says:

But each one is tempted when he is drawn away by his own desires and enticed. Then, when desire has conceived, it gives birth to sin; and sin, when it is full-grown, brings forth death.

Satan was drawn away by his own desire and his own pride to ascend above the throne of God (Isaiah 14:12–14). He wanted to be God. Because of this, he sinned and has been judged.

This is why Satan has been cast out of heaven and is reserved for hell for all eternity. Hell is separation from God and, moreover, His goodness. We know the beginning of Satan, and we know what will happen to him in the future — everlasting death apart from God's blessings.

*This is directed to Satan who was influencing the King of Tyre in Ezekiel.

Ezekiel 28:15; Isaiah 14:12-14

HOLY BIBLE

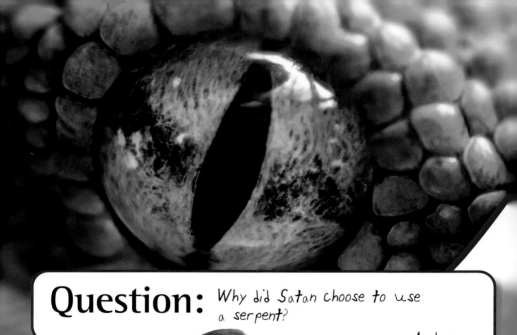

Question: Why did Satan choose to use a serpent?

Audrey

Age 10

26

Answer:

But I am afraid that just as Eve was deceived by the serpent's cunning, your minds may somehow be led astray from your sincere and pure devotion to Christ (2 Corinthians 11:3 ESV).

Satan's act of using a serpent may have been for several reasons. The Bible says the serpent was cunning — which means clever or smart.

When God made animals, they varied in their intelligence. In other words, some animals were clever, and some were not as clever. But all of them were created with the level of intelligence to perfectly do what they were created to do. For example, a platypus was created with the ability to swim and the intellect to do it properly. A chicken was not gifted with swimming, nor the intellect to do so!

The serpent was *more cunning* than other beasts of the field. So this may be one reason Satan used the serpent.

Another reason could be that the serpent originally had the ability to speak "phonically" or out loud. This was so that Satan could use the serpent to speak to Eve to try to deceive her.

Another possibility is that the serpent may have been the only animal near Eve when Satan decided to try to deceive her. There could be other reasons too.

Genesis 3:1;
Revelation 12:9, 20:2

27

Question: Can angels become demons?

Raymond

Age 11

28

Answer:

Now the Spirit expressly says that in latter times some will depart from the faith, giving heed to deceiving spirits and doctrines of demons (1 Timothy 4:1).

The Bible doesn't directly tell us that fallen angels became demons, but this is what most people believe. There are good reasons for this. When Satan fell, one-third of the angels joined his rebellion and fell. These spiritual beings now have a fallen and sinful nature.

Demons follow Satan (Matthew 12:25–28 — Beelzebub in this passage is one of Satan's names). Demons have an "unclean" or fallen nature and are spirits (e.g., Luke 4:33; 1 Timothy 4:1). Like the fallen angels, they will be tormented in hell when the time comes (Matthew 8:28, 25:41). As you can see, there is a good reason to view demons as fallen angels.

In the same way that Satan can have several names like the Devil, Lucifer, and Beelzebub, so fallen angels can also go by other names like demons, unclean spirits, and deceiving spirits. These names are often "interchangeable" with each other.

We don't have a problem calling fallen angels demons, deceiving spirits, and so on. The Bible talks about angels that did not rebel with Satan and chose to remain with God. We will discuss them in the next question.

Luke 11:18–20

29

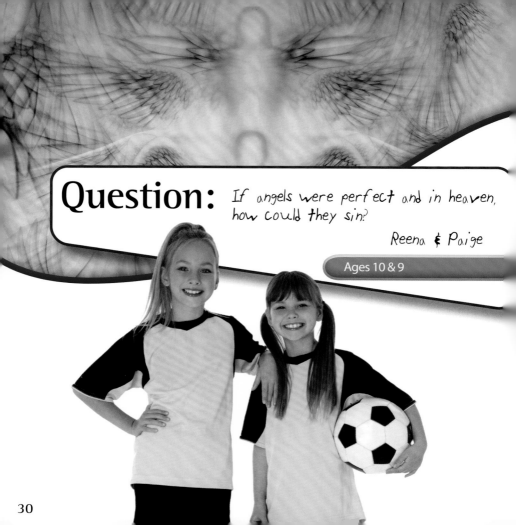

Question: If angels were perfect and in heaven, how could they sin?

Reena & Paige

Ages 10 & 9

Answer:

The devil, who deceived them, was cast into the lake of fire and brimstone where the beast and the false prophet are… (Revelation 20:10).

Like man, angels were given freedom to think and make decisions for themselves. Man had the option to obey God and refuse to eat from the Tree of the Knowledge of Good and Evil. Adam and Eve disobeyed God. They sinned, and we have to deal with the consequences of sin ever since it happened in the Garden of Eden about 6,000 years ago (Genesis 3).

Angels had the option to remain with God or follow after Satan when he rebelled against the Lord. Satan rebelled. Angels had the freedom to stand with God or disobey like Satan did.

One-third of the angels (Revelation 12:4) decided to follow Satan and rebel. And they must deal with the consequences. The angels that remained with God are called the "elect angels" (1 Timothy 5:21). These angels *elected* or "decided" to stay with God and oppose Satan and his angels. This means that two-thirds of the angels remained with God.

Fallen angels have no possibility of salvation. They tasted the heavenly gift of being with God and rebelled anyway. Man, being made in the image of God, has been given the means of salvation through Christ's death and Resurrection.

1 Timothy 5:21; Revelation 12:7

Question: If Satan sinned first, why did Adam get the blame?

Reena

Age 10

Answer:

Therefore, just as through one man sin entered the world, and death through sin, and thus death spread to all men, because all sinned (Romans 5:12).

Satan's sin was first but it only affected him. It didn't affect the world. The reason was because Satan was not given dominion over anything that God created.

Man was given "dominion" or "rule" over the earth and the animals in it, according to Genesis 1:26–27. In other words, man was put in charge of the earth, which included all the living creatures on the land, in the sea, and that flew in the air.

Satan turned to man, who did have dominion, to begin his deception with Eve. Then when Adam and Eve sinned, their whole dominion fell with them. This means the whole earth fell with Adam and Eve when they ate from the fruit. When Satan sinned, his sin didn't affect the earth.

But when Adam sinned, it affected everything of which they were put in charge. So the earth was affected and all the animals were affected by sin. Adam gets the blame for this, and the punishment for sin was death. Adam was put in charge of his wife, so he received the ultimate blame for sin in the world in Romans 5:12.

Genesis 1:26–27

Question: Do angels fight with demons?

Annie

Age 10

34

Answer:

And war broke out in heaven: Michael and his angels fought with the dragon; and the dragon and his angels fought (Revelation 12:7).

We can see from this verse in Revelation that angels indeed fight against rebellious angels. Fallen or evil angels are often equated with demons. Angels are spiritual beings (Hebrews 1:14). Because of this, we are limited in our understanding of these battles.

But we know that God wins. This means the fallen angels or demons do not win. Their ultimate punishment is the lake of fire or hell (Matthew 25:41). This doesn't mean that demons lose every battle (e.g., Acts 19:13–17). Just like battles in war, the enemies can have advances.

In the Bible, we see where demons had possessed people and Jesus had to rebuke them and send them away. It shows the power of Jesus over the beings that He created. Jesus conferred this power to His Apostles to drive out demons.

All of us have been called to resist the devil himself. If we submit to God and resist the devil, whose power has been broken by Jesus, he will flee (James 4:7). Angels and demons fight, but there is one winner — God — with the angels who fight with Him.

Matthew 25:41; James 4:7;
Jude 1:9

Question: If Satan knows he is going to lose, then why does he keep trying?

Noah

Age 10

36

Answer:

To the pure all things are pure, but to those who are defiled and unbelieving nothing is pure; but even their mind and conscience are defiled (Titus 1:15).

Satan is consumed with evil. As a result, he is no longer in his "right mind" because his own sin has corrupted or warped his mind. He knew what heaven was like with all of its goodness, but he rejected it because of his own pride. Now Satan's desire is to lash out at God and bring as many people down to hell as he can.

But they traded heaven for sin by betraying God. God knew they would sin. It didn't take God by surprise. Satan, fallen angels, and demons cannot change that sinful nature that they now have (i.e., *mind and conscience is defiled or "messed up"*).

With man's fallen nature, we can be changed and redeemed by Jesus Christ. We can once again be sanctified (made "holy" or "pure" by the Holy Spirit) because Christ's righteousness becomes our righteousness. It is transferred to us (Romans 4:22–24).

Because Satan has a fallen nature that will not be redeemed, his mind is warped and distorted and cannot realize that whatever he does, it will not thwart God. So his own fallen nature prevents him from being able to stop. Satan will no longer be an adversary to God and man when he is finally cast into hell (Revelation 20:10).

James 1:13–15

HOLY BIBLE

37

Question: What do the devil and demons look like?

Grant

Age 7

38

Answer:

You were the anointed cherub who covers; I established you; you were on the holy mountain of God; you walked back and forth in the midst of fiery stones (Ezekiel 28:14).

Very little is given in the Bible about the appearance of demons. This makes sense. Satan and demons are spiritual, so we don't really know what they would look like in the physical world.

We are given a brief description by God of cherubim, which are a spiritual type of "angels." This is how they would look if they were physical. They had a face and wings, for example. Satan was called an "anointed cherub" in Ezekiel 28:14. Thus, it is possible that the cherub description would also fit Satan, unless his spiritual appearance had changed due to sin and the Curse in Genesis 3.

When spiritual beings are described in human or physical terms, it is called "personification." This is often done to relate the nature of spiritual beings to man — like God having hands, a back, and a face (Exodus 33:20–23). The Bible tells us a lot about the actions of demons and the devil, but the Bible is silent on what these spiritual beings look like.

Exodus 33:20–23

39

Question: Did the serpent have legs?

Grace

Age 11

40

Answer:

So the LORD God said to the serpent: "Because you have done this, you are cursed more than all cattle, and more than every beast of the field; on your belly you shall go, and you shall eat dust all the days of your life (Genesis 3:14).

Animals, including the serpent, were cursed by God as a result of sin. In Genesis 3, we know that the serpent would crawl on its belly. The Bible doesn't say if the serpent originally had legs or not. Today, most serpents whether snakes, lizards, legless lizards, komodo dragons, or crocodiles, crawl on their belly.

Some of these animals have legs and some do not. Yet, all crawl on their bellies. Some think that the serpent had legs but was changed to have no legs. Some think its legs were merely shortened or changed. A few others think the serpent didn't have legs before or after the Curse. If the serpent was already crawling on its belly before the Curse, then what would the point of the Curse be?

So likely, it had legs originally, because there were other physical changes going on at the Curse as well. For example, some plants changed to have thorns and thistles and Eve (and all women after her) would have pain when having children. There were many physical changes occurring as a result of sin and the Curse.

Isaiah 65:25; Micah 7:17

41

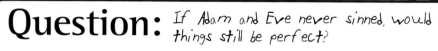

Question: If Adam and Eve never sinned, would things still be perfect?

Jackson

Age 9

42

Answer:

Therefore, just as through one man sin entered the world, and death through sin, and thus death spread to all men, because all sinned (Romans 5:12).

That is a great question! If Adam and Eve's descendants hadn't eaten either, then yes, things would still be perfect. But someone was bound to sin and eat the fruit of the Tree of the Knowledge of Good and Evil.

Keep in mind that God, who made man in His image, allowed man to freely choose (Genesis 2:16). Adam and Eve chose to eat and sinned against God (Genesis 3:6).

God knows all things (Psalm 147:5; Colossians 2:3). God already had a plan in place to save us even before Adam sinned. The Bible says Jesus was "slain from the foundation of the world" (Revelation 13:8). In other words, Jesus knew He would die on the Cross before Adam even sinned.

God always knew that man would sin and we would be in need of a Savior to save us from sin and death. Jesus died the death that we deserve for our sin. Jesus, being God, was able to satisfy God's wrath on sin. This is what makes salvation possible. No one else is capable of taking on the world's sin for *all* time except Jesus. Have you received Jesus Christ as Savior?

Genesis 2:16; Revelation 13:8

43

SATAN

Question: What was Satan's original name?

Tallia

Age 9

Answer:

Then Jesus said to him, "Away with you, Satan! For it is written, 'You shall worship the LORD your God, and Him only you shall serve'" (Matthew 4:10).

Satan goes by many names. So do we! We can go by our first name, middle name, or last name (Mr. Hodge or Mr. Ham, for example). Or we can go by nicknames or shortened names like Ken instead of Kenneth, Dave rather than David, Liz from Elizabeth, or Jon reduced from Jonathan.

Satan goes by other names too. One popular name is "the devil." Other names for Satan include ancient serpent/serpent of old (Revelation 12:9), Abaddon (destruction), Apollyon (destroyer) (Revelation 9:11), Beelzebub/Beelzebul (Matthew 12:27), Belial (2 Corinthians 6:15), and tempter (Matthew 4:3).

Satan is also called the "god of this world/age" (2 Corinthians 4:4), "ruler of this world" (John 12:31), and "father of lies" (John 8:44).

Another name for Satan is Lucifer which means "light bringer" or "Star of the Morning/Morning Star" in Isaiah 14:12. Some believe that Lucifer was a heavenly or angelic name that was taken from Satan when he rebelled. The Bible doesn't say this, so we have to be cautious about it. Even so, Jesus takes the title "Star of the Morning/Morning Star" away from Satan as it is used of Jesus in Revelation 22:16.

Isaiah 14:12; Revelation 22:16

45

Question: When we die, do we become angels?

Gershom

Age 8

46

Answer:

For if God did not spare the angels who sinned, but cast them down to hell and delivered them into chains of darkness, to be reserved for judgment (2 Peter 2:4).

It is a misconception that when people die, they become angels. Hebrews 12:22–23 points out that in the City of God, the heavenly Jerusalem, it has both angels and people [the "spirits of just men made perfect"]. When Christians, who are also called saints, die and go to heaven, we are finally made "perfect" — this means we no longer sin. In other words, perfected saints are there; but so are the angels of God. We are separate beings, so people do not become angels.

In certain ways, we will be like angels in heaven sharing in God's goodness directly. But we are still distinct. Remember that in the beginning, man was made a little lower than the angels (Psalm 8:5; 2 Peter 2:11). But we are also made in the image of God (Genesis 1:26–27), and for those in Christ who are saved and go to heaven, we are the "bride of Jesus Christ" who is the King of kings. This gives us a very high position. Saints are even put in charge of judging the world and angels (1 Corinthians 6:2–3; 2 Peter 2:4).

Psalm 8:5; 1 Corinthians 6:2–3

Answers Are Always Important!

The Bible is truly filled some amazing answers for some of our toughest faith questions. The Answers Book for Kids series answers questions from children around the world in this multi-volume series. Each volume will answer over 20 questions in a friendly and readable style appropriate for children 6–12 years old; and each cove a unique topic, including Creation and the Fall; Dinosaurs and the Flood of Noah; God and the Bible; Sin, Salvation, and the Christian Life; and more!

MASTERBOOKS.COM
— Where Faith Grows! —